W9-CMD-762

# THE HAMMARSKJÖLD FORUMS

*Case Studies*
*on*
*The Role of Law*
*in the*
*Settlement of International Disputes*

# The Cambodian Incursion . . .
# Legal Issues

*Proceedings of the Fifteenth Hammarskjöld Forum*

Donald T. Fox
*Editor*

Published for

The Association of the Bar of the City of New York

by

OCEANA PUBLICATIONS, INC.

Dobbs Ferry, N.Y.

1971

Library of Congress Catalog Card Number 79-141325
International Standard Book Number 0-379-11815-7

Printed in the United States of America

DEDICATED

TO

THE MEMORY OF

QUINCY WRIGHT

December 8, 1890 – October 17, 1970

# THE FIFTEENTH HAMMARSKJÖLD FORUM

May 28, 1970

Participants

William H. Rehnquist, Esq.
*Assistant Attorney General, Office of Legal Counsel,*
*U.S. Department of Justice*

Robert B. McKay, Esq.
*Dean, New York University School of Law*

John R. Stevenson, Esq.
*Legal Adviser, U.S. Department of State*

Abram Chayes, Esq.
*Professor of Law, Harvard University School of Law;*
*formerly Legal Adviser, U.S. Department of State*

John Carey, Esq.
*Special Committee on the Lawyer's Role in the Search for Peace*

# Table of Contents

Participants . . . . . . . . . . . . . . . . . . . .   v

Editor's Foreword   . . . . . . . . . . . . . . . .   xi

## Part One

## THE FORUM

Introduction by Andreas F. Lowenfeld   . . . . . . .   1

The Constitutional Issues — Administration Position: by
William H. Rehnquist   . . . . . . . . . . . . .   4

The Constitutional Issues  — Opposition position: by
Robert B. McKay   . . . . . . . . . . . . . . .   16

The International Law Issues — Administration Position:
by John R. Stevenson   . . . . . . . . . . . . .   24

The International Law Issues — Opposition Position: by
Abram Chayes   . . . . . . . . . . . . . . . .   34

Rebuttals . . . . . . . . . . . . . . . . . . . .   42

## Part Two

QUESTIONS AND STATEMENTS FROM THE FLOOR   47

## Part Three

## DOCUMENTARY SUPPLEMENT

*This supplement contains relevant sections of documents that are prominently mentioned in the foregoing discussions of United States involvement in Indochina.*

Constitution of the United States   . . . . . . . . .   57

Charter of the United Nations   . . . . . . . . . . .   58

Agreement of the Cessation of Hostilities in Cambodia (1954) . . . . . . . . . . . . . . . . . .  61

Final Declaration of Geneva Conference (1954) . . . .  63

Cease-Fire Agreements in Indochina: Statement of President Eisenhower (1954) . . . . . . . . . .  66

Statement of Under Secretary of State at Geneva Conference (1954) . . . . . . . . . . . .  67

Southeast Asia Collective Defense Treaty (1954) . . .  69

Gulf of Tonkin Resolution (1964) . . . . . . . . .  73

President Nixon's Address to the Nation on Southeast Asia (1970) . . . . . . . . . . . . . . . . . .  74

Yost Letter to the United Nations Security Council (1970)  76

Hatfield-McGovern: Amendment to the Military Procurement Bill . . . . . . . . . . . . .  78

SELECTED BIBLIOGRAPHY . . . . . . . . . .  79

# Editor's Foreword

The Eighth Hammarskjold Forum, held in October, 1965, addressed itself to the topic "The Southeast Asia Crisis." In his introduction to the proceedings of that Forum, Lyman M. Tondel, Jr. then Chairman of the Special Committee on the Lawyer's Role in the Search for Peace, mentioned that "emotions and frustrations were running high over the increasing involvement of the United States in Vietnam" and that some would have preferred to focus solely on that involvement. However, in line with the educational function of these forums a broader and hopefully constructive approach had been chosen.

With this approach, the Eighth Forum sought to look beyond Vietnam and beyond the war toward the possibility of developing a regional Mekong Community. The theme for the Forum's constructive orientation was established in the working paper prepared by Kenneth T. Young, Jr., former United States Ambassador to Thailand. Mr. Young's analysis proceeded from a view that had to be shared by all thoughtful people who believed in the possibility of a successful conclusion of the war: "It would have made no sense to become so heavily involved without either a strategic concept or a legal basis." In Mr. Young's view, the strategic concept was to set limits to the abuse of power by the Peking government beyond its national boundaries and to induce it to accommodate to a legally based world community. The legal basis for United States involvement was, he felt, firmly supported by the Southeast Asia Collective Defense Treaty of 1954, to which the Senate consented by a vote of 82-1; by the Tonkin Gulf Resolution adopted ten years later by a vote of 502-2; and, finally, by international law and the United Nations Charter.

A retrospective view of the 1965 Hammarskjold Forum reveals an intervening change in outlook. When the Fifteenth Hammarskjöld Forum was held on May 28, 1970, there did not seem to be a shared assumption that the Vietnam War was a burden the United States had to bear. Neither did any of the participants suggest that patience and wisdom could bring about a political settlement that would achieve the strategic objective articulated in 1965 by Ambassador Young. Instead of hopefully exploring a broad topic with an educational purpose, the Fifteenth Hammarskjold Forum focused on two specific issues: (i) the constitutionality of the President's ordering the invasion of Cambodia and of the proposal that Congress countermand this order by requiring a troop withdrawal; (ii) the appropriateness of such military action under principles of international law which seek to limit justifications for the use of armed force.

In introducing this Forum to the reader, it is worth relating two contemporaneous events that reflect the context in which it was held. At the conclusion of the Forum, a special meeting of the Association of the Bar was held, convened by petition and attended by a small percentage of the total membership, but not unusually small for a special meeting. Despite the tradition of not taking political action, at least in matters involving national policy, this meeting, by a vote of 197-64, resolved opposition to United States involvement in the war and urged immediate withdrawal of United States military forces. Also, about a week prior to the Forum, a convocation of lawyers opposed to United States military involvement in Indochina had been held at the House of the Association and was addressed by the President of the Association, the Mayor of New York City, a former Chief Justice of the United States and a former presiding Justice of the Appellate Division. On the following morning a delegation of some 500 lawyers traveled by special train to Washington where they called on selected Congressmen to urge support of bills designed to limit the ability of the President to continue the war. It should be noted that the lawyers voting on the resolution and those who took a day off from normal professional duties to lobby against the war included both young idealists and distinguished elder lawyers, some of whom had long believed in strong Presidential direction of national policy, particularly in the areas of security and foreign affairs, and had supported this theory through close collaboration with several administrations.

During this period a number of bills were introduced to reaffirm the role of Congress in the direction of foreign affairs. The Cooper-Church amendment to the Foreign Military Sales Act proposed to prohibit the use of funds for military operations in Cambodia after July 1, 1970, "[i]n concert with the declared objectives of the President" to conclude the operation by that date.

Although as so expressed this proposal was adopted by the Senate on June 30, it was not concurred in by the House. Ultimately, however, the House did accept a Senate rider to this bill which repealed the Gulf of Tonkin resolution.

When the Military Procurement Bill was reported to the Senate, the Hatfield-McGovern amendment was introduced to limit further expenditure of funds for operations in Indochina after December 31, 1970, or in Cambodia after 30 days from enactment and to require withdrawal of troops from Vietnam by June 30, 1971 unless expressly authorized by Congress. In modified form, requiring withdrawal by December 31, 1971, with a possible 60-day extension if the President deemed it necessary for the safety of American forces, this bill was defeated on September 1, 1970, by a vote of 39 for and 55 against. Major contributing factors to the defeat of the Hatfield-McGovern amendment were continuing doubts as to the wisdom of restricting the power of the President as Commander-in-Chief to protect American troops in Vietnam as well as observance of the announced July 1 deadline for American withdrawal from Cambodia and reaffirmation of the President's intention of continuing the disengagement from Vietnam.

Although the Fifteenth Hammarskjöld Forum was held in this context, it was not designed as part of the effort, in which members of the Association did participate, to influence the Administration to carry out a policy of disengagement in Southeast Asia. As prior Hammarskjöld Forums, it dealt with legal issues relevant to a current crisis in international affairs as part of a continuing effort to develop the lawyer's role in the search for peace. Its purpose was to elucidate the applicability of international law and constitutional law to the planning and execution of foreign policy. Hopefully, it will serve this end for the President's legal and foreign policy advisors and for all readers of this volume.

> Donald T. Fox, Chairman
> Special Committee on the Lawyer's
> Role in the Search for Peace
> The Association of the Bar
> of the City of New York

xiii

# The Forum

# HAMMARSKJÖLD FORUM: EXPANSION OF THE VIET NAM WAR INTO CAMBODIA— THE LEGAL ISSUES

*Soon after the President's announcement of movement of United States forces into Cambodia, a number of committees of the Association of the Bar of the City of New York agreed it would be useful to sponsor a discussion of the legal issues raised by this action. The discussion was held in the form of a debate at the House of the Association on May 28, 1970 under the auspices of the Hammarskjöld Forum. The debate, chaired by Mr. John Carey, was divided into the issues under the United States Constitution and the issues under international law, with one speaker representing each side followed by rebuttals and discussion from the floor. The entire debate, slightly edited, is reproduced below.*

## INTRODUCTION

### ANDREAS F. LOWENFELD

A LONG with the tragedy—and the many individual tragedies —of the expanded Indochina War, there are some interesting ironies. International law, which many thought dead at least as regards the security interests of the great powers, suddenly seems to have revived. The war is just as horrible, useful or useless, meaningful or meaningless at 107° E. as it is at 106° E. But the shock of crossing the vague and unmarked border between two states that hardly anyone had heard of twenty years ago and that did not exist twenty-five years ago, galvanizes a whole nation. After a period of declining protest, boredom and apparently a feeling that "Papa knows best," the country is transformed into a sea of protest, not only among the young and the radicals, but among many people who had never before protested anything. There were many factors, of course, and certainly the deaths at Kent State served to concentrate these feelings. But my impression is that no other kind of escalation—resumption of "search and destroy" operations, extended bombings in South or North Viet Nam, or support for the South Vietnamese government in its treatment of its critics—would have had the same effect as the march across an international boundary.

As the ensuing pages will show, the international law arguments of aggression, self-defense, sanctuary, invitation and consent, and so on, can be carried on at several levels of technical discussion. The reader can judge the outcome for himself. But now a public debate—not just in the House of the Association of the Bar but across the country—focuses upon international law as a moral question. I do not know how long it will last, and I call it an irony, not yet a benefit. But in my view it is worth a moment's pause.

Second, the country turns to Congress in a way not seen in the United States in forty years. The liberals—however one may define the term—now look to the legislature to protect them from what they regard as an overbearing Presidency (of both parties), whereas ever since Franklin Roosevelt a strong Presidency has meant "progress" and Congress has been thought of typically as conservative, out of touch, a collection of vested interests. Persons who in the past would have staunchly defended the maximum range of the President's power over foreign affairs, now favor amendments to deny all defense appropriations if United States troops are not out of Viet Nam or Cambodia by a certain date. I leave to the panelists the substantive discussion about the validity of such curbs under our constitutional system, or indeed about the relation among the branches of our government in the field of foreign affairs. I only want to point out that the political philosophy of many has changed and that the recent trend in our distribution of powers has been drawn into question.

I remember from my own experience in the State Department in the period 1961-1966 the recurring debates within the government whether a given action—the quarantine around Cuba, the landing in the Dominican Republic, the bombing of North Viet Nam, the dispatch of troops to South Viet Nam—should be accompanied or followed by a "legal brief." Those arguing in favor said, in effect, that not to publish a legal justification would leave the field to the critics, and might well give the impression in this country and elsewhere that the United States Government really did not care about law in international affairs. Those arguing against a legal brief said that by producing a "justification" for each of its actions the United States would debase law, particularly international law, fragile as that body of law already was. In large part, of course, the debate would depend on the quality of the briefs, which (allowing for some differences in the approach of the particular government lawyers) depended on the soundness of their client's case.

In class, the suggestion has been made more than once that if it is impossible to write a good brief, the action in question should

2

not be taken. No one, in my recollection, made that suggestion within the decision-making bodies of the United States Government concerning the major instances of employment of force. I do not make that suggestion here. I would no more delegate decision-making in international affairs to the lawyers than I would to soldiers or economists or historians. But I think the point is worth thinking about.

In this context the Association of the Bar of the City of New York has performed a real service. By announcing the Hammarskjöld Forum on Cambodia as soon as practicable after the President's announcement of the Cambodia campaign, the Association has prompted the government lawyers to decide whether to speak or to keep silent. Whatever the reader may think of the merits of each side's case, I think it is clear that professional discussion of the issues of constitutional and international law involved in the President's action contributes to public understanding of that action. It is too early to tell whether such discussion contributes to governmental decision-making as well.

# THE CONSTITUTIONAL ISSUES—
# ADMINISTRATION POSITION

WILLIAM H. REHNQUIST

I am pleased to avail myself of the opportunity of discussing the legal basis for the President's recent action in ordering American Armed Forces to attack Communist sanctuaries inside the border of Cambodia. So much of the discussion surrounding these recent events has been emotional that I think the Association of the Bar performs a genuine public service in encouraging reasoned debate of the very real issues involved.

I wish in these remarks to develop answers to several questions which I believe lie at the root of the matter under discussion. After having explored these questions in their historical context, I will make an effort to apply to the Cambodian incursion what seem to me to be the lessons of both history and constitutional law.

First, may the United States lawfully engage in armed hostilities with a foreign power in the absence of a congressional declaration of war? I believe that the only supportable answer to this question is "yes" in the light of our history and of our Constitution.

Second, is the constitutional designation of the President as Commander-in-Chief of the Armed Forces a grant of substantive authority, which gives him something more then just a seat of honor in a reviewing stand? Again, I believe that this question must be answered in the affirmative.

Third, what are the limits of the President's power as Commander-in-Chief, when that power is unsupported by congressional authorization or ratification of his acts? One would have to be bold indeed to assert a confident answer to this question. But I submit to you that one need not approach anything like the outer limits of the President's power, as defined by judicial decision and historical practice, in order to conclude that it supports the action that President Nixon took in Cambodia.

Before turning to a more detailed discussion of these three questions, let me advert briefly to the provisions of the Constitution itself with respect to the war power and to the debates of the Framers on this subject. Article I, section 8 provides that Congress shall have the power "to declare war." Article II, section 2 designates the President as Commander-in-Chief of the Armed Forces.

This textual allocation of authority readily suggests that a division of the nation's war power between the President and Congress was intended. An examination of the proceedings of the Constitutional Convention as found in the Madison notes confirms that suggestion.[1] The Framers did not intend to precisely delimit the boundary between the power of the executive branch and that of the legislative branch any more than they did in any of the other broad areas they considered. While rejecting the traditional power of kings to commit unwilling nations to war, they at the same time recognized the need for quick executive response to rapidly developing international situations.

It is interesting to note that the question before the Convention on Friday, August 17, 1787, was a motion to approve the language of the draft as it then read conferring upon Congress the power "to make war," rather than "to declare war."[2] During the debate, Charles Pinckney urged that the warmaking power be confined to the Senate alone, while Pierce Butler asked that the power be vested in the President. James Madison and Elbridge Gerry then jointly moved to substitute the word "declare" for the word "make," thus in their words "leaving to the Executive the power to repel sudden attacks." Rufus King supported the substitution of the word "declare," urging that the word "make" might be understood to mean to "conduct war," which he believed to be an executive function.

After this brief debate with only New Hampshire dissenting, it was agreed that the grant to Congress should be of the power to "declare" war. Pinckney's motion to strike out the whole clause, and thereby presumably leave the way open to vest the entire warmaking power in the Executive, was then defeated by a voice vote.[3]

The Framers here, as elsewhere in the Constitution, painted with a broad brush, and it has been left to nearly two hundred years of interpretation by each of the three coordinate branches of the National Government to define with somewhat more precision the line separating that which the President may do alone from that which he may do only with the assent of Congress.

It has been recognized from the earliest days of the Republic by the President, by Congress, and by the Supreme Court, that the United States may lawfully engage in armed hostilities with a foreign power without a congressional declaration of war. Our

---

[1] J. Madison, Notes of Debates in the Federal Convention of 1787, at 475-77 (Ohio Univ. Press ed. 1966).

[2] Id.

[3] Id.

history is replete with instances of "undeclared wars," from the war with France in 1798 through 1800, to the Vietnamese war. The Fifth Congress passed a law contained in the first book of the *Statutes at Large*, authorizing President Adams to "instruct the commanders of the public armed vessels which are, or which shall be employed in the service of the United States, to subdue, seize and take any armed French vessel, which shall be found within the jurisdictional limits of the United States, or elsewhere, on the high seas."[4] Now this is clearly an act of war, engaging American ships in armed hostilities, and yet Congress authorized it without feeling at all obligated to declare war on France.

The President proceeded to carry out congressional instructions, and such naval seizures were not uncommon during the period of the undeclared war with France. The Supreme Court, in a case arising out of this undeclared war, recognized the differences between what it called "solemn" war, which required a declaration by Congress, and "imperfect" war, which did not.[5]

Other examples abound of congressional authorization for armed military action without Congress having declared war. This does not answer the question, obviously, as to what the President may do without congressional authorization. The fact that the United States can engage in armed hostilities without congressional declaration of war does not mean that it can do so without congressional authorization. But it focuses on substance rather than form, and I think history simply will not admit any other conclusion than that a declaration of war by Congress is not necessary to legitimize the engagement of American Armed Forces in conflict.

What power does the designation of the President as Commander-in-Chief confer upon him? This type of question is one that for obvious reasons has not been the subject of a lot of judicial precedents so one has to pick his way among historical actions and among occasional observations by Supreme Court Justices in order to get some idea of what was intended. Chief Justice Marshall, writing for the Court in *Little v. Barreme*,[6] in 1804 spoke of the power of the President to order the seizure of a ship on the high seas in a situation where Congress has not specified the procedure:

It is by no means clear, that the President of the United States, whose high duty it is to "take care that the laws be faith-

---

[4] Act of July 9, 1798, ch. 67, 1 Stat. 578.
[5] Bas v. Tingy, 4 U.S. (4 Dall.) 36, 39-40 (1800).
[6] 6 U.S. (2 Cranch) 170 (1804).

6

fully executed," and who is commander-in-chief of the armies and navies of the United States, might not, without any special authority for that purpose, in the then existing state of things, have empowered the officers commanding the armed vessels of the United States, to seize and send into port for adjudication, American vessels which were forfeited, by being engaged in this illicit commerce.[7]

Justice Grier, speaking for the Supreme Court in its famous decision in the *Prize Cases*,[8] likewise viewed the President's designation as Commander-in-Chief as being a substantive source of authority on which he might rely:

Whether the President in fulfilling his duties, as Commander-in-chief, in suppressing an insurrection, has met with such armed hostile resistance, and a civil war of such alarming proportions as will compel him to accord to them the character of belligerents, is a question to be decided *by him*, and this Court must be governed by the decisions and acts of the political department of the Government to which this power was entrusted. "He must determine what degree of force the crisis demands."[9]

Lest it be thought that Chief Justice Marshall and Justice Grier are not relevant to the twentieth century, Justice Jackson, concurring in *Youngstown Sheet & Tube Co. v. Sawyer*,[10] expressed a similar thought:

We should not use this occasion to circumscribe, much less to contract, the lawful role of the President as Commander in Chief. I should indulge the widest latitude of interpretation to sustain his exclusive function to command the instruments of national force, at least when turned against the outside world for the security of our society.[11]

Presidents throughout the history of our country have exercised this power as Commander-in-Chief as if it did confer upon them substantive authority. They have deployed American Armed Forces outside of the United States. They have sent American Armed Forces into conflict with foreign powers on their own initiative. Presidents have likewise exercised the widest sort of authority in conducting armed conflicts already authorized by Congress.

These are actually, I believe, three separate facets of the President's power as Commander-in-Chief. They are the power to commit American Armed Forces to conflict where it hasn't

---

7 Id. at 176.
8 67 U.S. (2 Black) 635 (1862).
9 Id. at 670.
10 343 U.S. 579, 643 (1952).
11 Id. at 645.

previously existed, the power to deploy American Armed Forces throughout the world, frequently in a way which might invite retribution from unfriendly powers, and the power to determine how a war that's already in progress will be conducted.

Congress has on some of these occasions acquiesced in the President's action without formal ratification; on others it has ratified the President's action; and on still others it has taken no action at all. On several of the occasions, individual members of Congress, and, at the close of the Mexican War, one House of Congress on a preliminary vote, have protested executive use of the Armed Forces. While a particular course of executive conduct to which there was no opportunity for the legislative branch to effectively object cannot conclusively establish a constitutional precedent in the same manner as it would be established by an authoritative judicial decision, a long continued practice on the part of the Executive, acquiesced in by the Congress, is itself some evidence of the existence of constitutional authority to support such a practice. As stated by Justice Frankfurter in his concurring opinion in the *Youngstown Steel* case:

> The Constitution is a framework for government. Therefore the way the framework has consistently operated fairly establishes that it has operated according to its true nature. Deeply embedded traditional ways of conducting government cannot supplant the Constitution or legislation, but they give meaning to the words of the text or supply them.[12]

The historical examples have been marshalled in numerous recent studies of the President's power, and I will but summarize some of them briefly. President Jefferson, in 1801, sent a small squadron of American naval vessels into the Mediterranean to protect United States commerce against the Barbary pirates. He was of the view that for these ships to take offensive, as opposed to defensive, action, congressional action would be necessary.

In 1845 President Polk ordered military forces to the coast of Mexico and to the western frontier of Texas in order to prevent any interference by Mexico with the proposed annexation of Texas to the United States. Following annexation, Polk ordered General Zachary Taylor to march from the Nueces River which Mexico claimed as the southern border of Texas, to the Rio Grande River, which Texas claimed as her southern boundary, and beyond. While so engaged, Taylor's forces encountered Mexican troops, and hostilities between the two nations commenced on April 25, 1846.[13]

---

[12] Id. at 610.
[13] 1 S. Morison & H. Commager, The Growth of the American Republic 591-93 (4th ed. 1950).

There had been no prior authorization by Congress for Taylor's march south of the Nueces. Justice Grier, in his opinion in the *Prize Cases*, commented on the fact, stating: "The battles of Palo Alto and Resaca de la Palma had been fought before the passage of the Act of Congress of May 13, 1846, which recognized *'a state of war as existing by the act of the Republic of Mexico.'* "[14]

In 1854 President Pierce approved the action of the naval officer who bombarded Greytown, Nicaragua, in retaliation against a revolutionary government that refused to make reparations for damage and violence to United States citizens. This action was upheld by Judge Samuel Nelson, then a judge in the Southern District of New York and later a Justice of the Supreme Court of the United States, in *Durand v. Hollis*.[15] In his opinion in that case, Judge Nelson said:

> The question whether it was the duty of the president to interpose for the protection of the citizens at Greytown against an irresponsible and marauding community that had established itself there, was a public political question, in which the government, as well as the citizens whose interests were involved, was concerned, *and which belonged to the executive to determine*; and his decision is final and conclusive, and justified the defendant in the execution of his orders given through the secretary of the navy.[16]

In April 1861 President Lincoln called for 75,000 volunteers to suppress the rebellion by the Southern States,[17] and proclaimed a blockade of the Confederacy.[18] These actions were taken prior to their later ratification by Congress in July 1861.[19] The Supreme Court upheld the validity of the President's action in proclaiming a blockade in the *Prize Cases*.[20]

In 1900 President McKinley sent an expedition of 5000 United States troops as a component of an international force during the Boxer Rebellion in China.[21] While Congress recognized the existence of the conflict by providing for combat pay,[22] it neither declared war nor formally ratified the President's action.

Similar incidents in Central America took place under the administrations of Presidents Theodore Roosevelt,[23] Taft[24] and

---

14 67 U.S. (2 Black) at 668.
15 8 F. Cas. 111 (No. 4186) (C.C.S.D.N.Y. 1860).
16 Id. at 112 (emphasis added).
17 Morison & Commager, supra note 13, at 649.
18 Id. at 668-69.
19 Id at 669.
20 67 U.S. (2 Black) 635 (1862).
21 J. Rhodes, The McKinley & Roosevelt Administrations 127 (1922).
22 Id.
23 Morison & Commager, supra note 13, at 403-04.
24 M. Rodriguez, Central America 119 (1965).

Wilson.[25] Naval or armed forces were sent to Panama,[26] Nicaragua,[27] and twice to Mexico[28] in the first two decades of the twentieth century. On none of these occasions was there prior congressional authorization.

Prior to the Vietnam conflict, the most recent example of Presidential combat use of American forces without congressional declaration of war was President Truman's intervention in the Korean conflict. In many senses, this is undoubtedly the high water mark of executive exercise of the power of Commander-in-Chief to commit American forces to hostilities.

Following the invasion of South Korea by the North Koreans in June 1950 and a request for aid by the United Nations Security Council, President Truman ordered air and sea forces to give South Korean troops cover and support and ordered the Seventh Fleet to guard Formosa.[29] Ultimately 250,000 troops were engaged in the Korean War which lasted for more than three years.

President Truman relied upon the United Nations Charter as a basis for his action, as well as his power as Commander-in-Chief. The fact that his actions were authorized by the United Nations Charter, however, does not reduce the value of the incident as a precedent for executive action in committing United States Armed Forces to extensive hostilities without a formal declaration of war by Congress. The United Nations Charter was ratified by the Senate and has the status of a treaty, but it does not by virtue of this fact override any consitutional provision.[30] If a congressional declaration of war would be required in other circumstances to commit United States forces to hostilities to the extent and nature of those undertaken in Korea, the ratification of the United Nations Charter would not obviate a like requirement in the case of the Korean conflict.

Presidents have likewise used their authority as Commander-in-Chief to deploy United States forces throughout the world. Critics of President Wilson claimed that his action in arming American merchant vessels in early 1917 precipitated our entry into the First World War. Similarly, President Roosevelt's critics have asserted that various actions he took to aid the Allies in the year 1941 played a part in our involvement in the Second World

---

[25] Morison & Commager, supra note 13, at 442-43.

[26] Id. at 403-04.

[27] Id. at 438-39.

[28] Id. at 442-43.

[29] R. Morris, Great Presidential Decisions 400 (1965).

[30] See Reid v. Covert, 351 U.S. 487 (1956); Geofroy v. Riggs, 133 U.S. 258 (1890).

War. Whatever substance there may be to these criticisms, these Presidential actions stand as the constructions placed by these two Presidents on their power as Commander-in-Chief of the Armed Forces.

The third facet of the power of Commander-in-Chief is the right and obligation to determine how hostilities, once lawfully begun, shall be conducted. This aspect of the President's power is one which is freely conceded by even those students who read the Commander-in-Chief provision least expansively. Indeed, it has seldom, if ever, been seriously challenged. Chief Justice Chase, concurring in *Ex parte Milligan*,[31] said:

> Congress has the power not only to raise and support and govern armies but to declare war. It has, therefore, the power to provide by law for carrying on war. This power necessarily extends to all legislation essential to the prosecution of war with vigor and success, *except such as interferes with the command of the forces and the conduct of campaigns. That power and duty belongs to the President as commander-in-chief.*[32]

And if we look back at several of our armed engagements in the past, whether declared wars or otherwise, this type of decision has been freely and frequently engaged in by the Commander-in-Chief. In the First World War, for example, it was necessary to make the tactical decision whether the United States troops in France would fight as a separate command under a United States general or whether United States divisions should be incorporated in existing groups or armies commanded by French or British generals. President Wilson and his military advisors decided that United States forces would fight as a separate command.

In the Second World War similar military decisions on a global scale were required—decisions that partook as much of political strategy as they did of military strategy. For example, should the United States concentrate its military and material resources on either the Atlantic or Pacific fronts to the exclusion of the other, or should it pursue the war on both fronts simultaneously? Where should the reconquest of Allied territories in Europe and Africa begin? What should be the goal of the Allied powers? It will readily be recalled by many of us that decisions such as these were reached by the Allied commanders and chief executive officers of the Allied nations without any formal congressional participation. The series of conferences attended by President Roosevelt and President Truman ultimately established

---

[31] 71 U.S. (4 Wall.) 2 (1866).
[32] Id. at 139 (emphasis added).

the Allied goals in fighting the Second World War, including the demand for unconditional surrender on the part of the Axis nations.

Similar strategic and tactical decisions were involved in the undeclared Korean War. Decisions such as whether the United States forces should pursue Korean forces into North Korea and as to whether United States Air Force planes should pursue Communist planes north of the Yalu River into China were made by the President as Commander-in-Chief without formal congressional participation.

While these examples help outline the contours of the President's power as Commander-in-Chief in the absence of congressional authorization, they do not, of course, mark a sharp boundary. It is abundantly clear, however, that Congress can by authorizing Presidential action remove any doubt as to its constitutional validity. Thus, when the Gulf of Tonkin Resolution was enacted,[33] Congress noted that whatever the limits of the President's authority in acting alone might be, whenever the Congress and the President act together "there can be no doubt" of his constitutional authority.[34]

Congress may, of course, authorize Presidential action by declaration of war, but its authorization may also take other forms. From the example of the Fifth Congress' delegation to President Adams of the power to stop French vessels on the high seas,[35] through the legislative acts authorizing President Eisenhower to use troops in Lebanon[36] and in Formosa[37] and authorizing President Kennedy to use Armed Forces in connection with the Cuban missile crisis,[38] to the Gulf of Tonkin Resolution in 1964,[39] both Congress and the President have made it clear that it is the substance of congressional authorization, and not the form which that authorization takes, which determines the extent to which Congress has exercised its portion of the war power.

It has been suggested that there may be a question of unlawful delegation of powers here, and that Congress is not free to give a blank check to the President. Whatever may be the answer to that abstract question in the domestic field, I think it is

---

[33] Act of Aug. 10, 1964, Pub. L. No. 88-408, 78 Stat. 384. See Documentary Supplement infra.

[34] H.R. Rep. No. 1708, 88th Cong., 2d Sess. 4 (1965).

[35] See text accompanying note 4 supra.

[36] Act of Mar. 9, 1957, Pub. L. No. 85-7, 71 Stat. 5.

[37] Act of Jan. 29, 1955, Pub. L. No. 84-4, 69 Stat. 5.

[38] Act of Oct. 3, 1962, Pub. L. No. 87-733, 75 Stat. 697.

[39] Act of Aug. 10, 1964, Pub. L. No. 88-408, 78 Stat. 384. See Documentary Supplement infra.

plain from *United States v. Curtiss-Wright Export Corp.*,[40] which was decided only a year after *Schechter Poultry Corp. v. United States*,[41] that the principle of unlawful delegation of powers does not apply in the field of external affairs. The Supreme Court in *Curtiss-Wright* made this clear:

> Whether, if the Joint Resolution had related solely to internal affairs it would be open to the challenge that it constituted an unlawful delegation of legislative power to the Executive, we find it unnecessary to determine. The whole aim of the resolution is to affect a situation entirely external to the United States, and falling within the category of foreign affairs.
>
> . . . .
>
> It results that the investment of the federal government with the powers of external sovereignty did not depend upon the affirmative grants of the Constitution. The powers to declare and wage war, to conclude peace, to make treaties, to maintain diplomatic relations with other sovereignties, if they had never been mentioned in the Constitution, would have vested in the federal government as necessary concomitants of nationality.[42]

The situation confronting President Nixon in Viet Nam in 1970 must be evaluated against almost two centuries of historical construction of the constitutional division of the war power between the President and Congress. It must also be evaluated against the events which had occurred in the preceding six years. In August 1964 at the request of President Johnson following an attack on American naval vessels in the Gulf of Tonkin, Congress passed the so-called Gulf of Tonkin Resolution. That resolution approved and supported the determination of the President "to take all necessary measures to repel any armed attack against the forces of the United States and to prevent further aggression." It also provided that the United States is "prepared as the President determines, to take all necessary steps, including the use of armed force, to assist any member or protocol state of the Southeast Asia Collective Defense Treaty requesting assistance in defense of its freedom."[43]

While the legislative history surrounding the Gulf of Tonkin Resolution may be cited for a number of varying interpretations of exactly what Congress was authorizing, it cannot be fairly disputed that substantial military operations in support of the

[40] 299 U.S. 304 (1936).

[41] 295 U.S. 495 (1935). In that case the Supreme Court had declared that Congress was not permitted to abdicate or to delegate to the President its domestic economic powers under the Constitution. Id. at 529.

[42] 299 U.S. at 315, 318.

[43] Act of Aug. 10, 1964, Pub. L. No. 88-408, 78 Stat. 384. See Documentary Supplement infra.

South Vietnamese were thereby authorized. Steadily increasing numbers of United States Armed Forces were sent into the Vietnamese combat during the years following the passage of the Gulf of Tonkin Resolution. United States Air Force planes bombed not only South Viet Nam, but North Viet Nam. When President Nixon took office in January 1969, he found nearly half a million combat and supporting troops engaged in the field in Viet Nam. His predecessor, acting under the authorization of the Gulf of Tonkin Resolution, had placed these troops in the field, and I for one have no serious doubt that Congress and the President together had exercised their shared war power to lawfully bring about this situation.

President Nixon continued to maintain United States troops in the field in South Viet Nam in pursuance of his policy to seek a negotiated peace which will protect the right of the South Vietnamese people to self-determination. He has begun troop withdrawals, but hostile engagements with the enemy continue. The President feels, and I believe rightfully, that he has an obligation as Commander-in-Chief to take what steps he deems necessary to assure the safety of American Armed Forces in the field. On the basis of the information avaliable to him, he concluded that the continuing build-up of North Vietnamese troops in sanctuaries across the Cambodian border posed an increasing threat both to the safety of American forces and to the ultimate success of the Vietnamization program. He also determined that, from a tactical point of view, combined American-South Vietnamese strikes at these sanctuaries had a very substantial likelihood of success. He, therefore, ordered them to be made.

The President's determination to authorize incursion into these Cambodian border areas is precisely the sort of tactical decision traditionally confided to the Commander-in-Chief in the conduct of armed conflict. From the time of the drafting of the Constitution it has been clear that the Commander-in-Chief has authority to take prompt action to protect American lives in situations involving hostilities. Faced with a substantial troop commitment to such hostilities made by the previous Chief Executive, and approved by successive Congresses, President Nixon had an obligation as Commander-in-Chief of the Armed Forces to take what steps he deemed necessary to assure their safety in the field. A decision to cross the Cambodian border, with at least the tacit consent of the Cambodian Government, in order to destroy sanctuaries being utilized by North Vietnamese in violation of Cambodia's neutrality, is wholly consistent with that obligation. It is a decision made during the course of an armed conflict already commenced as to how that conflict will be conducted, rather than a determination that some new and previously unauthorized military venture will be taken.

By crossing the Cambodian border to attack sanctuaries used by the enemy, the United States has in no sense gone to "war" with Cambodia. United States forces are fighting with or in support of Cambodian troops, and not against them. Whatever protest may have been uttered by the Cambodian Government was obviously the most perfunctory, formal sort of declaration. The Cambodian incursion has not resulted in a previously uncommitted nation joining the ranks of our enemies, but instead has enabled us to more effectively deter enemy aggression heretofore conducted from the Cambodian sanctuaries.

Since even those authorities least inclined to a broad construction of the executive power concede that the Commander-in-Chief provision does confer substantive authority over the manner in which hostilities are conducted, the President's decision to invade and destroy the border sanctuaries in Cambodia was clearly authorized under even a narrow reading of his power as Commander-in-Chief.

# THE CONSTITUTIONAL ISSUES—
# OPPOSITION POSITION

ROBERT B. McKAY

It is tempting to dwell on a theme of misplaced empire and wars that are lost at home without being won abroad. But we who are lawyers must resist the urge for passionate response to a world gone mad. There are significant legal issues, both constitutional and international, that transcend the moment. These questions are important enough and difficult enough to merit all the rational skills that lawyers can bring to their solution. Today in this Forum we seek no less than to define the powers of President and Congress in the context of war in fact. What can the President do alone? What can the Congress do alone? And what is forbidden to each without the approval of the other?

I have of late often differed with our President, but I must agree with his conclusion that when the action is hot the rhetoric must remain cool, and I express to you now my admiration for his deputy, Mr. Rehnquist, who has kept the rhetoric very cool indeed. I find to my pleasure that he and I read the same Constitution, in general even the same clauses. We read the same history, and in large part we come up with the same interpretation. I agree with a great deal of what Mr. Rehnquist has said, at least two-thirds of it. That is, I would answer affirmatively, as he does, his first two questions, "May the United States engage in hostilities without a declaration of war?" Of course; it has been done many times. "Is the Commander-in-Chief power committed to the President by the Constitution one of substance?" Of course. Our differences relate only to the definition of the limits of Presidential power.

Accordingly, I shall confine my remarks to an analysis of the vital national debate on the powers of President and Congress in connection with warlike activities. Let me begin with some general observations. In a democracy such as ours the power of effective government—or the art of government, if you prefer—is a fragile thing. In this context Americans tend to think first of the Constitution. The written Constitution, however, is only the tip of the iceberg. Separation of powers, here a central issue, is nowhere referred to in the Constitution in so many words. The United States is governed not only in accordance with formal, written principles of constitutional law, but as well by an unwritten Constitution of at least equal significance.

It is for this reason that we should not expect to find absolute answers to questions that lie near the center of the uncharted area. Indeed, many believe that in this very flexibility reposes the genius and the durability of the American constitutional system. To agree to all of this, however, is not at all to concede that no answers are discoverable. In the words of the Constitution, however spare, an important beginning is revealed. Commentary contemporaneous with the drafting of the Constitution, developing practice, and judicial decision provide a richness of texture that answers many questions.

The Presidential power stems from several clauses in Article II. These clauses provide that "[t]he executive Power shall be vested in a President";[1] that "he shall take Care that the Laws be faithfully executed";[2] that he "shall be Commander in Chief of the Army and Navy of the United States";[3] and that "[h]e shall have Power, by and with the Advice and Consent of the Senate, to make Treaties."[4]

Debates in the Constitutional Convention show that the decision to make the President Commander-in-Chief was intended to accomplish two objectives. The first aim was to insure civilian control over the military forces of the nation. As Alexander Hamilton interpreted the power, it "would amount to nothing more than the supreme command and direction of the military forces, as first General and Admiral of the Confederacy."[5]

The importance of civilian control at the top has often been demonstrated, nowhere more dramatically than when President Truman removed from military command the popular war hero, General Douglas MacArthur. And the President said, with chararteristic simplicity: "I could do nothing else and still be President of the United States."[6]

The second objective was to confer on the President some restraint against a potentially war-minded legislature. In the Constitutional Convention, for example, Mason argued that the purse and the sword must not be in the same hands.[7] But clearly, the President's power to check the Congress was not conversely intended to give him a power beyond congressional restraint.

The catalogue of congressional powers in section 8 of article I is impressive. Congress is given the power to "lay and collect

---

[1] U.S. Const. art. II, § 1. See Documentary Supplement infra.
[2] U.S. Const. art. II, § 3. See Documentary Supplement infra.
[3] U.S. Const. art. II, § 2. See Documentary Supplement infra.
[4] Id.
[5] The Federalist No. 69, at 430 (H. Lodge ed. 1888) (A. Hamilton).
[6] See L. Koenig, The Chief Executive 243 (1964).
[7] 2 M. Farrand, Records of the Federal Convention 319 (1911).

Taxes . . . to provide for the common Defence and general Welfare of the United States"; "to declare war" (the only power that Mr. Rehnquist mentioned); "to raise and support armies," with the important qualification that "no Appropriation of Money to that use shall be for a longer Term than two Years"; "To provide and maintain a Navy"; "to make Rules for the Government and Regulation of the land and naval Forces"; "to control and regulate the militia"; and "to make all Laws which shall be necessary and proper for carrying into Execution the foregoing Powers and all other Powers vested by this Constitution in the Government of the United States, or any Department or Officer thereof."[8]

Debate in the Constitutional Convention on this subject confirms the intent of the Framers to give to Congress ultimate control over the power to wage war as well as the formal power to declare war.[9] The instrumentalities for the effective exercise of this power were as varied as the needs that might arise. At the minimum the Framers would have viewed an appropriation limited to the provision of funds necessary for the withdrawal of troops as a proper exercise of that power. Parliament had exercised such a power in 1678,[10] and it was the conscious design of the drafters of the Constitution to give Congress more power over foreign affairs and over warmaking than the Parliament had possessed.

Justice Jackson, concurring in the *Youngstown Steel* case,[11] made the point in these words: "[The President] has no monopoly of 'war powers,' whatever they are. While Congress cannot deprive the President of the command of the army and navy, only Congress can provide him an army and navy to command."[12]

Originally, it may have seemed that the most important of the enumerated congressional powers was that to declare war. Although twentieth-century usage may have dimmed the practical significance of the clause, the debate in the Convention is revealing as to the intended division of authority between President and Congress. As originally drafted, the clause empowered Congress "to make war." Some delegates believed that the power should lie with the Executive as it did in England. But most of the Convention seemed convinced that the power should lie with Congress, leaving to the President the power to defend against sudden attack. Accordingly, the Convention decided to "insert

---

8 U.S. Const. art. I, § 8.
9 See Farrand, supra note 7, at 313-19.
10 E. Wade & G. Phillips, Constitutional Law 152 (2d ed. 1935).
11 Youngstown Sheet & Tube Co. v. Sawyer, 343 U.S. 579, 634 (1952).
12 Id. at 644.

'declare,' striking out 'make' war, leaving to the executive the power to repel sudden attack."[13]

Thus, it seems fair to say that the Framers had in mind a division of functions. The President, as Commander-in-Chief, was charged with the conduct of hostilities after the war had been legally begun. He was also expected to take measures to repel any actual attack upon the United States as an incident of his executive power and his power as Commander-in-Chief. But the power to initiate hostilities in ordinary circumstances was clearly meant to be reserved to the Congress. "Thus, the President, unless his veto is overridden, may prevent war, but he cannot constitutionally act alone to begin a war."[14]

Early practice was entirely consistent with this understanding. When President John Adams was confronted with growing naval hostilities with France at the end of the eighteenth century, Alexander Hamilton advised that "[i]n so delicate a case, in one which invokes so important a consequence as that of war, my opinion is that no doubtful authority ought to be exercised by the President."[15] Adams followed that advice.[16] Similarly, in 1801 when President Jefferson faced hostilities on the Barbary Coast, he concluded that he should authorize only defensive measures unless Congress should approve the commitment of forces for offensive action.

This notion of congressional initiative in the warmaking functions was observed in practice until well into the twentieth century, with only a single important exception in the nineteenth century. During the early weeks of the Civil War, President Lincoln imposed military conscription, suspended the writ of habeas corpus in certain portions of the country and imposed a blockade of Southern ports.[17] Congress was not in session at the time, and Lincoln did not hasten to convene it. But later Congress in effect ratified all the President's acts,[18] as indeed was necessary for their enforceability. Surely the conscription call would not have withstood challenge. Even the congressional habeas corpus legislation barely survived wartime challenges, only to be

[13] See J. Madison, Notes of Debates in the Federal Convention of 1787, at 475-77 (Ohio Univ. Press ed. 1966).

[14] See 116 Cong. Rec. S7117 (daily ed. May 13, 1970) (remarks of Senator McGovern) (emphasis omitted).

[15] See Wormuth, The Vietnam War: The President Versus the Congress, in The Vietnam War and International Law 22 (R. Falk ed. 1968).

[16] See Act of June 13, 1798, ch. 53, 1 Stat. 565, and Act of Feb. 9, 1799, ch. 2, 1 Stat. 613, where Congress suspended commercial activity with France.

[17] See text accompanying note 20 infra.

[18] C. Swisher, American Constitutional Development 303 (2d ed. 1954)

severely limited after the close of hostilities in *Ex parte Milligan*.[19] And the blockade of the Southern ports was sustained in the *Prize Cases*[20] only because of the after-the-fact ratification by Congress, and even then only by a vote of five to four. The majority rationalized this limited approval of the action with this dictum:

> The greatest of civil wars was not gradually developed. . . . [I]t . . . sprung forth suddenly from the parent brain, a Minerva in the full panoply of war. The President was bound to meet it in the shape it presented itself, without waiting for Congress to baptize it with a name. . . .[21]

No comparably drastic Presidential initiative was asserted until the action of President Nixon in the sending of troops into Cambodia in 1970. President Lincoln, for example, was surely not unmindful of the superiority of congressional power in the total scheme of things. He may not have urged congressional participation as early as we think he should have, but he did seek, and he did secure, its approval for the unilateral action he had taken in response to the emergency that he thought confronted the country. He could hardly have failed to consult Congress in view of his own earlier position when a Congressman. After the conclusion of the Mexican War, for which the congressional declaration of war was secured after the beginning of hostilities, Congressman Lincoln joined in a House resolution which icily noted that General Taylor had won "a war unnecessarily and unconstitutionally begun by the President of the United States."[22]

There have been, it is true, a number of instances in which American Presidents have ordered armed forces into action outside the United States in response to various crises, real or imagined. And none would deny the vital necessity, particularly during the atomic age, of preserving the flexibility essential to permit immediate response to a sudden attack. But this important power must be subject to significant qualifications. Once the President has taken a decisive initiative, whether it constitutes war de facto or not, the Congress cannot be denied the power of deciding from the facts as it finds them whether to formalize the situation into a declared war, whether to approve the Presidential action by supporting legislation even without a formal declaration or whether to order withdrawal. If the Congress were instead required to execute and enforce the acts of the President by imple-

---

19 71 U.S. (4 Wall.) 2 (1866).
20 67 U.S. (2 Black) 635 (1863).
21 Id. at 668-69.
22 Cong. Globe, 30th Cong., 1st Sess. 95 (1848).

menting legislation, including monetary appropriations, that would reverse the roles of the executive and the legislative branches. It is after all the President who is required to "take care that the laws be faithfully executed." It is not the Congress that is charged with the "faithful execution" of the acts of the President.

It is not to the point to say that there have been minor skirmishes, or even mini-wars, in which the President has dispatched troops for some presumed need to protect the neutrality of American lives or property. However questionable may have been the wisdom of some of those Presidential decisions, and however little restraint the Congress has placed upon Presidential power in these circumstances, the balance of power prescribed in the Constitution has not changed.

Since the Civil War there have been two instances, and only two, in which a major warlike activity has been initiated by a President without congressional authority. One is the Korean War, as I am perfectly willing to call it; and the other is the war in Southeast Asia, which we can no longer describe as narrowly as we once did as the war in Viet Nam.

In the case of the Korean War President Truman acted in response to an attack upon a country which he believed the United States was committed to protect under outstanding treaty obligations. But in two respects the case differs from the recent Cambodian invasion. In Korea there was an invasion by a hostile power, and the President's action was immediately supported by the Security Council of the United Nations.[23] Neither of these conditions prevails in Cambodia. The issue rather is whether Congress has the authority to assert its constitutional power over the "Government and Regulation of the land and naval Forces,"[24] and through its appropriation power to require an orderly withdrawal of American forces.

Although I am prepared to argue that the President acted improperly in ordering the movement of troops into Cambodia, it is not necessary to assert that position in order to sustain the power of Congress to take whatever action it believes is necessary to affect the conduct of the war now in progress. If Congress has the power to declare war and to wage war, surely it cannot be denied the authority to put to an end a war that Congress believes does not serve the national interest. As Chief Justice Marshall

---

[23] U.N. Doc. S/1501 (1950).
[24] U.S. Const. art. I, § 8.

21

observed in 1801, the "whole powers of war" were "vested in congress."[25]

The short of it is, as it seems to me, that in these days of national and international peril the Constitution provides a secure shelter against unwanted war through its assurance that the United States will not go to war, or at least will not continue at war, over the expressed objection of *either* the President or the Congress.

The necessity for concurrence of legislative and executive judgment has been confirmed as well by the Supreme Court in matters arising out of the war power, even in contexts less dangerous than the act of war itself. Thus, in the *Youngstown Steel* case the Supreme Court denied the power of the President to seize and operate certain steel mills during the Korean War in the absence of congressional authorization.[26] The defect was, in Justice Black's opinion, that "the President's order does not direct that a congressional policy be executed in a manner prescribed by Congress—it directs that a presidential policy be executed in a manner prescribed by the President."[27] Thus, the *Youngstown Steel* case makes the point that where the President acts without direct constitutional authority or without legislative authority from Congress, he acts at his and the nation's peril. Somewhat similarly, in 1959 the Court invalidated a Defense Department order that was part of the federal loyalty-security program, applying a strict construction standard to the power of the executive branch to implement a policy which required legislative action under the powers of Congress.[28]

If Congress has sometimes in the past been more indulgent with Presidential assertions of authority than might be strictly necessary, this probably indicated in most cases congressional approval—or at least confidence in the judgment of the President with more information at his disposal—and an agreed sense of national purpose. Thus, nearly every past instance of "Presidential action" reflects, in my view, essential conjunction of executive and legislative intent and consensus of the public at large. But even if this was not true in every instance, there is no case to be made for surrender by Congress of its functions—both representative and legislative.

Finally, I come to the only point that Mr. Rehnquist chose to argue, the validity of the President's action in ordering Armed Forces of the United States into Cambodia. Successful conduct

---

25 The Amelia, 5 U.S. (1 Cranch) 1, 28 (1801).
26 Youngstown Sheet & Tube Co. v. Sawyer, 343 U.S. 579 (1952).
27 Id. at 588.
28 Greene v. McElroy, 360 U.S. 474 (1959).

of our government under the Constitution depends on faithful adherence by the principal parties to two vital "understandings" that undergird the system. Each of these was in my judgment violated by the President's action in Cambodia.

*First.* Major decisions of the President should be made only after consultation with, and expression of support from, congressional leadership. This necessity is underscored in the area of foreign policy, and it is doubly underscored where invasion of, or even entry into, another nation is contemplated—with or without invitation by that nation's leadership. This is the informal protection developed in practice to reinforce the stated congressional power to declare war. The difficulty with the formal authority is that it has become in practice a theoretical rather than a real safeguard; the formal check on the Executive has apparently been found to be too inflexible an arrangement. Unfortunately, the recent action of the President has endangered this delicate balance.

*Second.* The President should not take any action disapproved by a majority, or even by a substantial minority of the people without congressional approval. The limits of Presidential power are set by the principle of consensus—more difficult, more time-consuming than unilateral action—but ultimately essential to success. The reasons for the consensus rule should be clear—if not by logic, then by experience. The consequence of failing to work within the flexible boundaries set by consensus is substantial discontent and disharmony in American society. Evidence of that discontent abounds. We—and I include the President of the United States—ignore the dangers of that disharmony at peril to the nation.

# THE INTERNATIONAL LAW ISSUES—
# ADMINISTRATION POSITION

## JOHN R. STEVENSON

I welcome the opportunity to present the Administration's views on the questions of international law arising out of the current South Vietnamese and United States operations in Cambodia.[1] I do not intend to review in any detail the legal justification of earlier actions by the United States in Viet Nam. In 1966 the previous Administration set forth at some length the legal justifications for our involvement in South Viet Nam and our bombing of North Viet Nam.[2] In general, reliance was placed squarely upon the inherent right of individual and collective self-defense, recognized by Article 51 of the United Nations Charter. This legal case involved the showing that North Viet Nam had raised the level of its subversion and infiltration into South Viet Nam to that of an "armed attack" in late 1964 when it first sent regular units of its Armed Forces into South Viet Nam. The build-up of American forces in South Viet Nam and the bombing of North Viet Nam were justified as appropriate measures of collective self-defense against that armed attack.[3]

The legal case presented by the previous Administration was vigorously attacked and defended by various scholars of the international legal community.[4] Many of the differences rested on disputed questions of fact which could not be proved conclusively. This Administration, however, has no desire to re-argue those issues or the legality of those actions which are now history. In January 1969 President Nixon inherited a situation in which one-half million American troops were engaged in combat in South Viet Nam, helping the Republic of Viet Nam to defend itself against a

---

[1] The views of the Administration on the military and political issues have been expressed clearly by the President and other officials. See, in particular, President Nixon's address of April 30, 1970, reprinted in Documentary Supplement infra, and his press conference of May 8, N.Y. Times, May 9, 1970, at 8, col. 1. See also Deputy Secretary of Defense Packard's address of May 15, 1970 in Fort Worth, Texas.

[2] Meeker, The Legality of United States Participation in the Defense of Viet-Nam, submitted to the Senate Committee on Foreign Relations on March 8, 1966, 54 Dep't State Bull. 474 (1966).

[3] They were also justified on that basis in United States reports to the United Nations, pursuant to Article 51. See the texts of the letters from Ambassador Stevenson to the Security Council, dated February 7 and February 27, 1965, 52 Dep't State Bull. 240, 419 (1965).

[4] See the articles in The Viet-Nam War and International Law (R. Falk ed. 1968).

continuing armed attack by North Viet Nam. Our efforts have been to extricate ourselves from this situation by negotiated settlement if possible, or, if a settlement providing the South Vietnamese people the right of self-determination cannot be negotiated, then through the process of Vietnamization.[5] The current actions in Cambodia should be viewed as part of the President's effort to withdraw United States forces from combat in Southeast Asia.[6]

I appreciate this opportunity to discuss the questions of international law arising out of our actions in Cambodia. It is important for the Government of the United States to explain the legal basis for its actions, not merely to pay proper respect to the law, but also because the precedent created by the use of Armed Forces in Cambodia by the United States can be affected significantly by our legal rationale. I am sure you recall the choice that was made during the Cuban missile crisis in 1962 to base our "quarantine" of Cuba not on self-defense since no "armed attack" had occurred, but on the special powers of the Organization of American States as a regional organization under Chapter VIII of the United Nations Charter.[7] Within a narrower scope the arguments we make can affect the applicability of the Cambodian precedent to other situations in the future. I believe the United States has a strong interest in developing rules of international law that limit claimed rights to use armed force and encourage the peaceful resolution of disputes.

One way to have limited the effects of the Cambodian action would have been to obtain the advance, express request of the Government of Cambodia for our military actions on Cambodian territory. This might well have been possible.[8] However, had we

---

[5] The President reviewed our efforts at negotiation and the progress of Vietnamization in his statement of April 20, 1970, 62 Dep't State Bull. 603 (1970); he stated: "Our overriding objective is a political solution that reflects the will of the South Vietnamese people and allows them to determine their future without outside interference." Id. at 604.

[6] In announcing the use of force in Cambodia, President Nixon said: "We take this action not for the purpose of expanding the war into Cambodia but for the purpose of ending the war in Vietnam, and winning the just peace we all desire. We have made and will continue to make every possible effort to end this war through negotiation at the conference table rather than through more fighting in the battlefield." N.Y. Times, May 1, 1970, at 2, col. 4.

[7] See Chayes, Law and Quarantine of Cuba, 41 Foreign Affairs 550 (1963).

[8] On May 1, a Cambodian spokesman said that "the Cambodian Government as a neutral government [cannot] approve foreign intervention." However, on May 5, the Cambodian Government issued the following statement:

In his message to the American nation of 30 April, 1970, the President of the United States of America, Richard Nixon made public important measures which he had taken to oppose the growing military aggression of North Viet Nam on the territory of Laos, Cambodia and South Viet

done so, we would have compromised the neutrality of the Cambodian Government and moved much closer to a situation in which the United States was committing its Armed Forces to help Cambodia defend itself against the North Vietnamese attack. We did not wish to see Cambodia become a co-belligerent along with South Viet Nam and the United States. We are convinced that the interests of the United States, the Republic of Viet Nam, and Cambodia, and indeed the interests of all Asian countries, will best be served by the maintenance of Cambodian neutrality, even though that neutrality may be only partially respected by North Viet Nam.

As the President has made clear, the purpose of our Armed Forces in Cambodia is not to help defend the Government of Cambodia, but rather to help defend South Viet Nam and United States troops in South Viet Nam from the continuing North Vietnamese armed attack.[9] This limited purpose is consistent with the Nixon Doctrine, first set forth by the President at Guam on July 25, 1969,[10] that the nations of the region have the primary responsibility of providing the manpower for their defense.

The North Vietnamese have continued to press their attack against South Viet Nam since 1964 and have made increasing use of Cambodian territory in the furtherance of that attack. They have used Cambodia as a sanctuary for moving and storing sup-

---

Nam. One of these measures concerned aid of the United States of America in the defense of the neutrality of Cambodia, violated by the North Vietnamese.

The Salvation Government notes with satisfaction that the president of the United States of America has taken into account in his decision the legitimate aspirations of the Cambodian people which desires [sic] only to live in peace, in its territorial integrity, in its independence, and in its strict neutrality. For that reason, the Government of Cambodia wishes to declare that it respects the sentiments of President Richard Nixon in his message of 30 April, 1970 and expresses its gratitude for them.

It is high time now that the other friendly nations understand the extremely grave situation in which Cambodia finds herself and come to the aid of the Cambodian people, victims of armed aggression. The Salvation Government renews on this occasion its appeal for help issued 14 April, 1970, and points out that it will accept all unconditional help from friendly countries in all forms (military, economic and diplomatic).

N.Y. Times, May 5, 1970, at 16, col. 8.

[9] This is to be distinguished from the furnishing of weapons and ammunition to Cambodia pursuant to the Foreign Assistance Act, 22 U.S.C. §§ 2161-2410 (Supp. IV, 1969), amending 22 U.S.C. §§ 2161-2407 (1964), which is done to improve the ability of Cambodia to defend itself.

[10] The President's statements were not for direct quotation, but the New York Times of July 26, 1969 contains a fair summary of his remarks. N.Y. Times, July 26, 1969, at 1, col. 1. The President later clarified the Doctrine in his address to the nation on Viet Nam of November 3, 1969, N.Y. Times, Nov. 4, 1969, at 16, col. 1, and in his Report to the Congress dated February 18, 1970 on U.S. Foreign Policy for the 1970's. 116 Cong. Rec. 11,925 (daily ed. Feb. 18, 1970).

plies, for training, regrouping and resting their troops and as a center of their command and communications network. I assume that these facts are generally accepted, but it might be useful to give a few examples.

In the past five years, 150,000 enemy troops have been infiltrated into South Viet Nam through Cambodia. In 1969 alone, 60,000 of their military forces moved in from Cambodia. The trails inside Cambodia are used not only for the infiltration of troops but also for the movement of supplies. A significant quantity of the military supplies that support these forces came through Cambodian ports.

Since 1968 the enemy has been moving supplies through southern Cambodia to its forces in the Mekong Delta. Further, in the spring and summer of 1969, three to four regiments of regular North Vietnamese troops used Cambodian territory to infiltrate into the Mekong Delta. Up to that time, there had been no regular North Vietnamese combat units operating in this area.

As many as 40,000 North Vietnamese and Viet Cong troops were operating out of the Cambodian base areas against South Viet Nam prior to April 30. As the war in South Viet Nam intensified, Viet Cong and North Vietnamese troops have resorted more frequently to these sanctuaries and to attacking from them to avoid detection by or combat with United States and South Vietnamese forces.

During 1968 and 1969 the Cambodian bases adjacent to the South Vietnamese provinces of Tay Ninh, Pleiku, and Kontum have served as staging areas for regimental-size Communist forces for at least three series of major engagements—the 1968 Tet offensive, the May 1968 offensive and the post-Tet 1969 offensive.

Many of these North Vietnamese actions violate Cambodian neutrality. The generally accepted principles flowing from the Second Hague Convention of 1907[11] are that a neutral may not allow belligerents to move troops or supplies across its territory, to maintain military installations on its territory, or to regroup forces on its territory. A neutral is obligated to take positive action to prevent such abuse of its neutrality either by attempting to expel the belligerent forces or to intern them.

As a legal matter it is clear that a neutral must take active measures commensurate with its power to protect its territory from abuse by a belligerent. It is likewise clear that a neutral's

[11] 2 Am. J. of Int'l L. 117-27 (Official Doc. Supp. 1908).

"duty of prevention is not absolute, but according to his power."[12] Both the previous Cambodian Government under Prince Sihanouk and the present Government headed by Lon Nol have made efforts to limit, if not prevent, these violations of Cambodia's rights as a neutral. While the Sihanouk Government did not, in our judgment, do all that it should have done under international law, it unquestionably made some efforts. In any event, however, the control and restraint exercised by the previous Cambodian Government was progressively eroded by constant North Vietnamese pressure. Prior to the ouster of Prince Sihanouk, arms and munitions were regularly supplied to the North Vietnamese through the Port of Sihanoukville.

After the change of government on March 18, 1970 in which the United States was not involved in any respect, Cambodian police and other officials were driven out of many localities in the border area. When it became apparent to North Viet Nam that the new Cambodian Government was not willing to permit the same wide scope of unneutral use of its territory by North Vietnamese forces as the previous government, the decision was evidently taken to expel all Cambodian Government presence from the border areas and move militarily against the Cambodian army, with a view to linking up all the sanctuaries and the Port of Sihanoukville. This would have produced a unified and protected sanctuary from the Gulf of Siam along the entire border of South Viet Nam to Laos, with virtually unrestricted movement and unlimited supply access. The threat posed by such a situation of renewed and increased attacks against United States and Vietnamese troops in South Viet Nam is obvious. We also knew that enemy forces were instructed to emphasize attacks on United States forces and to increase American casualties.

That was the rapidly developing situation the President faced at the time of his April 30 decision to make limited military incursions into the Cambodian sanctuaries which had been militarily occupied by North Viet Nam. It was impossible for the Cambodian Government to take action itself to prevent these violations of its neutral rights. Its efforts to do so had led to the expulsion of its forces. In these circumstances, the question arises: What are the rights of those who suffer from these violations of Cambodian neutrality?

---

[12] As the Harvard Research Study in International Law pointed out in its 1939 Draft Convention on Rights and Duties of Neutral States in Naval and Aerial War, "[a] neutral State is not an insurer of the fulfillment of its neutral duties. It is obligated merely to 'use the means at its disposal' to secure the fulfillment of its duties." 33 Am. J. Int'l L. 247 (Supp. 1939).

It is the view of some scholars that when the traditional diplomatic remedy of a claim for compensation would not adequately compensate a belligerent injured by a neutral's failure to prevent illegal use of its territory by another belligerent, the injured belligerent has the right of self-help to prevent the hostile use of the neutral's territory to its prejudice.[13] Professor Castrén, the distinguished Finnish member of the International Law Commission, has stated: "If, however, a neutral State has neither the desire nor the power to interfere and the situation is serious, other belligerents may resort to self-help."[14] The more conservative view is that a belligerent may take reasonable action against another belligerent violating the neutral's territory only when required to do so in self-defense.[15]

The *United States Department of the Army Field Manual* relating to the law of land warfare states the following rule: "Should the neutral State be unable, or fail for any reason, to prevent violations of its neutrality by the troops of one belligerent entering or passing through its territory, the other belligerent may be justified in attacking the enemy forces on this territory."[16] This rule can be traced to, among others, the decision of the Greco-German Mixed Arbitral Tribunal after the First World War which had to deal with the German bombardment of Salonika

---

13 See M. Greenspan, The Modern Law of Land Warfare 538 (1959): "Should a violation of neutral territory occur through the complaisance of the neutral state, or because of its inability, through weakness or otherwise, to resist such violation, then a belligerent which is prejudiced by the violation is entitled to take measures to redress the situation, including, if necessary, attack on enemy forces in the neutral territory."

14 E. Castrén, The Present Law of War and Neutrality 442 (1954). See also II P. Guggenheim, Traité de Droit International Publique 346 (1954).

15 2 L. Oppenheim, International Law 698 (7th ed. 1952). This is true whether or not the neutral has met its obligations to use the means at its disposal to oppose belligerent use of its territory. J. Stone, Legal Controls of International Conflict 401 (1954) says: "One clear principle is that, the right of self-preservation apart, an aggrieved State is clearly not entitled to violate the neutral's territorial integrity, simply because his enemy has done so. Diplomatic representations and claim are the proper course." A Columbia Law Review Note concludes: "Military action within neutral territory may be justified as a measure of self-defense or as an appropriate response to the failure of a neutral state to prevent the use of its territory by belligerent forces . . . . It is suggested . . . that international law should permit and encourage primary reliance on self-defense as a justification." Note, International Law and Military Operations Against Insurgents on Neutral Territory, 68 Colum. L. Rev. 1127, 1147 (1968). See also Corfu Channel Case, [1949] I.C.J. 1, 34-35 (judgment of the court), 68, 77 (Krylov, J., dissenting).

16 FM 27-10, para. 520, at 185 (July 1956). Similar provisions were contained in the U.S. Rules of Land Warfare of 1940, para. 366, and in the British Manual of Military Law, para. 655. See M. Greenspan, The Modern Law of Land Warfare 538 n.23 (1959).

in Greece. During the war the Allied forces had occupied Salonika despite Greece's neutrality and the Germans responded with a bombardment. The Tribunal stated that Allied occupation constituted a violation of the neutrality of Greece, and that it was immaterial whether the Greek Government protested against that occupation or whether it expressly or tacitly consented to it. The Tribunal then concluded that "in either case the occupation of Salonika was, as regards Germany, an illicit act which authorized her to take, even on Greek territory, any acts of war necessary for her defense."[17]

In 1940 the British navy entered the territorial waters of then neutral Norway to liberate British prisoners on the *Altmark*, a German prison vessel. A thorough analysis of that action by Professor Waldock led him to the conclusion that in some circumstances a breach of neutrality by one belligerent threatens the security of the other belligerent in such a way that nothing but the immediate cessation of the breach will suffice. "Accordingly," wrote Professor Waldock, "where material prejudice to a belligerent's interests will result from its continuance, the principle of self-preservation would appear fully to justify intervention in neutral waters."[18]

As far back as the eighteenth century, DeVattel had this to say:

On the other hand, it is certain that, if my neighbour offers a retreat to my enemies, when they have been defeated and are too weak to escape me, *and allows them time to recover and to watch for an opportunity of making a fresh attack upon my territory . . .* [this is] inconsistent with neutrality . . . . [H]e should . . . not allow them to lie in wait to make a fresh attack upon me; *otherwise he warrants me in pursuing them into his territory.* This is what happens when Nations are not in a position to make their territory respected. It soon becomes the seat of the war; armies march, camp, and fight in it, as in a country open to all comers.[19]

The United States itself has sometimes in the past found it necessary to take action on neutral territory in order to protect itself against hostile operations. Professor Hyde cites many such instances of which I would note General Jackson's incursion into Spanish West Florida in 1818 in order to check attacks by Sem-

---

[17] Coenca Bros. v. The German State (1927) translated in H. Briggs, The Law of Nations: Cases, Documents and Notes 756-58 (1938).

[18] Waldock, The Release of the Altmark's Prisoners, 24 Brit. Y.B. of Int'l L. 216, 235-36 (1947). See also R. Tucker, The Law of War and Neutrality at Sea, XLX Int'l L. Studies 262 (1955).

[19] 3 E. DeVattel, Le Droit des Gens, bk. II § 133, at 277 (Fenwick transl. 1916) (emphasis added).

inole Indians on United States positions in Georgia; the action taken against adventurers occupying Amelia Island in 1817, when Spain was unable to exercise control over it; and the expedition against Francisco Villa in 1916, after his attacks on American territory which Mexico had been unable to prevent.[20]

I have summarized these precedents and the views of scholars and governments principally to show general recognition of the need to provide a lawful and effective remedy to a belligerent harmed by its enemy's violations of a neutral's rights. I would not suggest that those incidents and statements by themselves provide an adequate basis for analysis of the present state of the law. We all recognize that, whatever the merits of these views prior to 1945, the adoption of the United Nations Charter changed the situation by imposing new and important limitations on the use of armed force.[21] However, they are surely authority for the proposition that, assuming the Charter's standards are met, a belligerent may take action on a neutral's territory to prevent violation by another belligerent of the neutral's neutrality which the neutral cannot or will not prevent, providing such action is required in self-defense.

In general, under the United Nations Charter the use of armed force is prohibited except as authorized by the United Nations or by a regional organization within the scope of its competence under Chapter VIII of the Charter, or, where the Security Council has not acted, in individual or collective self-defense against an armed attack. It is this latter basis on which we rely for our actions against North Vietnamese Armed Forces and bases in Cambodia.

Since 1965 we and the Republic of Viet Nam have been engaged in collective measures of self-defense against an armed attack from North Viet Nam. Increasingly since that time the territory of Cambodia has been used by North Viet Nam as a base of military operations to carry out that attack, and it long ago reached a level that would have justified us in taking appropriate measures of self-defense on the territory of Cambodia. However, except for scattered instances of returning fire across the border, we refrained until April from taking such action in Cambodia. The right was available to us, but we refrained from exercising it in the hope that Cambodia would be able to impose greater restraints on enemy use of its territory. However, in late April a new and more dangerous situation developed. It became

---

20 1 C. Hyde, International Law 240-44 (2d ed. 1945).
21 See U.N. Charter art. 2, para. 4.

apparent that North Viet Nam was proceeding rapidly to remove all remaining restraints on its use of Cambodian territory to continue the armed attacks on South Viet Nam and our armed forces there.

Prior to undertaking military action the United States explored to the fullest other means of peaceful settlement. We awaited without success the outcome of the Cambodian Government's efforts to negotiate agreed limitations on the use of Cambodian territory by the North Vietnamese and the Viet Cong. We have continually tried in the Paris talks to bring about serious negotiation of the issues involved in the war. Soundings in the Security Council indicated very little interest in taking up the North Vietnamese violations of Cambodian territorial integrity and neutrality. We welcomed the French proposal looking to the possibility of an international conference, although not publicly for fear of discouraging Hanoi's participation. The Soviet Union, after initially indicating interest, backed away. We were particularly pleased with the calling of the Djakarta Conference of interested Asian states to deal with the Cambodian problem on a regional basis. The best long-run approach to East Asian security problems lies through cooperative actions such as this. In the short run, however, they cannot be expected to provide an adequate defense to the North Vietnamese military threat.

The United States has imposed severe limits on the activities of its forces. They will remain in Cambodia only a limited time— not beyond July 1, in a limited area—not beyond twenty-one miles from the border and with a limited purpose—to capture or destroy North Vietnamese supplies, to destroy base installations and to disrupt communications. To the maximum extent possible, we have directed our forces at enemy base areas and have tried to avoid civilian population centers. We have limited our area of operations to that part of Cambodia from which Cambodian authority had been eliminated and which was occupied by the North Vietnamese.

The Cambodian Government and the Cambodian people are not the targets of our operations. During the period from 1967 to 1970 the Cambodian Government became increasingly outspoken in its opposition to the North Vietnamese occupation. In fact, Prince Sihanouk's purpose in going to the Soviet Union and China when he was deposed was to solicit their help in persuading the North Vietnamese to get out of Cambodia. The Lon Nol Government has expressed its understanding of our actions.[22]

---

[22] See note 8 supra.

Our actions in Cambodia are appropriate measures of legitimate collective self-defense, and we have so reported to the United Nations, as required by Article 51 of the United Nations Charter.[23]

[23] U.N. Doc. S/9781 (1970). See Documentary Supplement infra.

# THE INTERNATIONAL LAW ISSUES—
# OPPOSITION POSITION

### ABRAM CHAYES

IN our polity the gravest acts of state inevitably have a major legal dimension. The tradition of our profession—indeed a measure of its right to be called a profession—is to insist that such acts be subjected not alone to the judgment of the political forum or to the test of success or failure but to professional scrutiny by professional peers. All our great debates have therefore been in part legal debates. We are engaged in one now. The Hammarskjöld Forum and the Association of the Bar discharge an important public duty by providing, as they have in the past, a setting in which these questions can be pursued with the seriousness and rigor that is their due.

On another such occasion, after the Cuban missile crisis, when I sat in the office John Stevenson now occupies, I said:

> International lawyers . . . have a responsibility for the kind of questions which they permit to be put as legitimate professional questions. One is often struck at the generality and abstraction of questions thought appropriate for discussion by scholars and publicists of international law and as well as by the Euclidean majesty of the discussion. "Was the quarantine legal?" A question put in that form is bound to elicit over-generalized and useless answers. The object of a first-year law school education is to teach students not to ask such questions.[1]

I am prepared to stand by that conclusion even though I am now on the other side of the fence. You will all, I think, understand the basis of that view. When we, as lawyers, make judgments about the "legality" of a client's course of action—although we seldom use that word—it is not a matter of sweeping application of some abstract norm. We narrow our focus by elaborate and detailed statement of the factual setting. We speak in the context of a specific procedural and remedial system for determining rights and obligation, and above all in the knowledge that courts sit and are available ultimately to give determinate and binding answers to our questions. In such a setting it is possible to give a responsible opinion that a deduction is allowable, or a passage in a prospectus is insufficient, or a particular school

---

[1] Proceedings of the Am. Soc'y of Int'l L., 57th Annual Meeting 11 (1963).

system is unconstitutional. In international law this setting is absent; it is distorting even to conduct the analysis as if procedures, remedies and courts were available. So I continue to believe that absolute judgments about "legality" used now are inappropriate in this debate, though I recognize that this puts me in opposition to many of my international law colleagues.

Having said this, it does not at all follow that international law and international legal analysis have no bearing on decisions like the missile crisis or the invasion of Cambodia, or on our own appraisal of them. On the contrary, the basis for Presidential decision would be seriously incomplete if it did not include a full analysis of the legal setting of the proposed action and judgment of that action would be inadequate without an examination of the relevant legal materials.

The decision to send American troops across an international boundary into Cambodia must be considered, as must every military action in foreign territory, in the light of the United Nations Charter, and in particular the provisions of Article 2(4):

All members shall refrain in their international relations from the threat or use of force against the territorial integrity or political independence of any state, or in any other manner inconsistent with the purposes of the United Nations.

Before examining these provisions in more detail, however, we should note that treaties and agreements to which the United States has adhered establish a special and more particularized regime for the area in question. Chief among these are the Geneva Accords of 1954[2] and the South East Asia Collective Defense Treaty (SEATO).[3]

The Final Declaration of the Geneva Conference of 1954 provides in paragraph 12 that each member of the Conference "undertakes to respect the sovereignty, the independence, the unity, and the territorial integrity of [Cambodia, Laos and Viet Nam] and to refrain from interference in their internal affairs."[4] The United States did not join in the Final Declaration, but it made a separate declaration of its own, taking note of the cease-fire agreements and the first twelve paragraphs of the Final Declaration.[5] With regard to these paragraphs the United States said that "it will refrain from the threat or use of forces to disturb them in accordance with Article 2(4) of the Charter of the United

---

[2] 31 Dep't State Bull. 164 (1954). See Documentary Supplement infra.

[3] Sept. 8, 1954, [1955] 6 U.S.T. 81, T.I.A.S. No. 3170. See Documentary Supplement infra.

[4] 31 Dep't State Bull. 164 (1954). See Documentary Supplement infra.

[5] Id. at 163. See Documentary Supplement infra.

Nations." As a result, the United States undertook an express and specific obligation not to disturb the sovereignty, independence, unity or territorial integrity of Cambodia, or to interfere in its internal affairs by threat or use of force.

It is true that North Viet Nam also undertook such an express and specific obligation, for it participated in the Final Declaration at Geneva. On the facts as we know them, North Viet Nam has not observed that obligation, and has in fact systematically violated it. I do not think, however, the United States can claim that North Viet Nam's breach, in this case, releases the obligation of the United States. These are not in form or in fact mutual and reciprocal obligations. They stand as independent declarations, particularly that of the United States, and the obligations they establish flow to the Indo-Chinese States, Cambodia, Laos and Viet Nam, as well as to the other declarers, who are therefore entitled to be consulted, at least, about change in that obligation. The United States took that view of the matter with respect to South Viet Nam in the State Department Memorandum of March 8, 1965 on the Legal Basis for United States Actions against North Viet Nam.[6] The Memorandum argues that breaches of the Accords by North Viet Nam "justify South Viet Nam to withhold its compliance with those provisions of the Accords which limit its ability to protect its very existence." The provisions referred to are those of the 1954 cease-fire agreement—which incidentally *was* a reciprocal agreement as between North and South—that limited recourse to foreign military assistance. United States action in support of South Viet Nam was justified indirectly by the request of the South Vietnamese Government rather than directly by the breach of North Viet Nam. In the present case there is no suggestion prior to the United States attack that Cambodia had taken the occasion of North Vietnamese incursions to invite the assistance of the United States.

In its declaration of 1954, the United States also said that "it would view any renewal of the aggression in violation of the aforesaid agreements with grave concern and as seriously threatening international peace and security." At the same time, President Eisenhower said: "The United States is actively pursuing discussions with other free nations with a view to the rapid organization of a collective defense in Southeast Asia in order to prevent further direct or indirect Communist aggression in that general area."[7] Two months later the SEATO Treaty was

---

[6] Department of State, Office of the Legal Adviser, Legality of the United States Participation in the Defense of Vietnam, 60 Am. J. Int'l L. 565-85 (1966).

[7] 31 Dep't State Bull. 163 (1954). See Documentary Supplement infra.

signed.[8] Because of its origin it can be regarded as a specific expression of United States security interests in the area. Moreover, it has been repeatedly cited by American officials as justifying and even requiring the United States military action in Viet Nam.

The Treaty creates a typical collective self-defense arrangement, modeled after the NATO and the Rio Treaties.[9] The operative provisions are in article IV, which distinguishes between "aggression by means of armed attack in the treaty area" covered by article IV(1), and "threats or dangers to the peace of the area other than by armed attack," dealt with in article IV(2). In the first case, "[e]ach party . . . agrees that it will in that event act to meet the common danger in accordance with its constitutional processes." In the second case, "the Parties shall consult immediately in order to agree on measures which should be taken for the common defense."

A number of grave problems arise in any attempt to invoke these provisions in relation to the Cambodian invasion. There was certainly no consultation with the Parties as required by article IV(2). Also it is doubtful whether the situation existing before the invasion can be characterized as an armed attack within the meaning of article IV(1). That phrase has been narrowly construed in United States treaty practice. In the Cuban missile crisis, for example, the Rio Treaty was invoked under article 6, dealing with situations other than armed attack, rather than article 3, dealing with armed attack. The concept is surely not more expansive than the meaning of armed attack embodied in Article 51 of the United Nations Charter, to which we shall turn in a moment, and it may be narrower.

In my view there is yet another and an even more difficult objection to application of the SEATO Treaty framework to the Cambodian invasion. Cambodia is what is known as a Protocol State under the Treaty—that is a state not a party to the Treaty but to whose territory the parties agreed to extend the provisions of article IV. Article IV(3) expressly provides, however, that "no action on the territory of any [Protocol] State shall be taken except at the invitation or with the consent of the government concerned."

It is admitted that there was no invitation or consent in advance of the United States invasion. In fact, the first reaction of the Cambodian government was to oppose the United States

---

8 Sept. 8, 1954, [1955] 6 U.S.T. 81, T.I.A.S. No. 3170. See Documentary Supplement infra.

9 The North Atlantic Treaty, Apr. 4, 1949, art. 5, para. 1, 63 Stat. 2241 (1949), T.I.A.S. No. 1964; Interamerican Treaty of Reciprocal Assistance, Sept. 2, 1947, art. 3, para. 1, 62 Stat. 168 (1948), T.I.A.S. No. 1838.

and South Vietnamese move. More recently there have been some expressions by the Lon Nol government that may be taken as inviting or requesting further military help from the United States and as acquiescing in its actions thus far. These statements, in my view, must be treated with the deepest reserve, in view of the circumstances in which they were made—*i.e.*, by a weak, new government, hardly capable of free sovereign expression, beset by three invasions at once and forced by circumstances to choose among them.

Article IV(3) and the treatment of Protocol States under SEATO have an important bearing on the scope of individual and collective self-defense available to the parties to the Treaty in the area. The provisions of article IV show that the parties contemplated that attacks on a Protocol State or armed action based on its territory might be armed attacks or threats within the meaning of paragraphs (1) and (2) of the article. Nevertheless, they limited the range of available defensive responses to such acts or threats by expressly foregoing action upon the territory of a Protocol State without its consent or invitation.

Let us turn now to consider the right of individual and collective self-defense referred to in Article 51 of the United Nations Charter. In the closest thing to a legal defense of the Cambodian action before this afternoon, the United States has invoked this concept. Ambassador Yost's letter to the President of the Security Council, dated May 5, five days after the invasion, says that the attacks on Cambodia were "appropriate measures of collective self-defense by the armed forces of the Republic of Viet Nam and the United States of America."[10]

Although the letter does not cite article 51, it is clear from the phraseology and argumentation used that that article is relied upon to take the action out of the prohibition against the threat or use of force in article 2(4). Article 51 refers to "the inherent right of individual or collective self-defense *if an armed attack occurs.*" The analysis must focus on the concept of "armed attack." In general this has been thought to cover a very narrow range of sudden threats requiring instantaneous response before the collective processes of the United Nations or other international agencies could be invoked. In commenting upon the *Caroline* incident, Daniel Webster, the then Secretary of State, insisted that the necessity for self-defense, especially when the measures involve a neutral party, must be "instant, overwhelming, and leaving no choice of means."[11] As Mr. Stevenson noted, the United States

---

[10] U.N. Doc. S/9781 (1970). See Documentary Supplement infra.
[11] 2 J. Moore, A Digest of International Law § 217, at 412 (1906).

did not treat the emplacement of missiles in Cuba as an armed attack within the meaning of article 51.[12] Some have argued for a loose construction of the concept to permit preemptive action in the context of a threat of attack with nuclear weapons, but these were not present in Cambodia.

None of the facts adduced by the United States or by the President supports, in my view, the conclusion that there was at the time of the invasion an armed attack against Viet Nam from Cambodia, as opposed, perhaps to preparations for an attack some time in the future. Certainly nothing suggests that the threat was instant and overwhelming, leaving no choice of means of response. On the contrary, Ambassador Yosts' letter recites that the North Vietnamese bases in Cambodia had been maintained for five years, without, presumably, requiring a United States or South Vietnamese military response. The letter recites a number of recent changes in the situation, but on the whole they comprise North Vietnamese movements westward toward Pnom Penh or laterally along the border rather than eastward toward the United States positions. The most Ambassador Yost is prepared to contend is that "North Viet Nam . . . is concentrating its main force in these base areas in *preparation for further* massive attacks into South Viet Nam."[13] There is no suggestion in this letter or in any other documentation of an urgency precluding international consultation. One is forced to the conclusion that failure to invoke the processes of the international community was a consequence not of urgent necessity, but of inconvenience, or more likely of the anticipation that such consultation would not produce an endorsement of the military action. But then one could hardly expect the President to consult his allies or to submit his decision to the scrutiny of international processes of review when apparently he consulted only briefly with his chief cabinet officers and was unwilling to submit to the scrutiny of Congress.

A further point about Ambassador Yost's letter should be discussed. It says that the measures

> being taken by United States *and* South Viet-Namese forces are restricted in extent, purpose and time. They are confined to the border areas. . . . Their purpose is to destroy the stocks and communications equipment that are being used in aggression against the Republic of Viet-Nam. When that purpose is accomplished our forces and those of the Republic of Viet-Nam will promptly withdraw.[14]

---

12 See Stevenson, Hammarskjöld Forum, 45 N.Y.U.L. Rev. 628, 649 (1970).
13 U.N. Doc. S/9781 (1970) (emphasis added). See Documentary Supplement infra.
14 Id. (emphasis added).

These recitals of the limited character of the military action are integral to the self-defense justification in Ambassador Yost's letter. The letter was written on May 5. Three weeks later, it appears that those limits will not be observed, particularly as regards South Vietnamese troops. If so, it seems to me not only is the basis of the May 5 letter undermined, but the triviality and lack of seriousness with which the international law problems were treated by the Administration are exposed.

If, as I have argued, we are not entitled to make absolute judgments about what international law *required* in the situation, we can ask and answer another question: Were the actions and conduct of the United States in this situation appropriate on the part of a nation that holds itself out as exemplar and defender of the rule of law in world affairs? I have no hesitancy in saying that the actions and conduct of the United States do not meet that standard. Among the basic items of evidence for that conclusion is that until this meeting, a month after the invasion, the Administration had not even attempted a comprehensive and systematic justification of its position at international law.

More basically, I think we are entitled to hold the United States to a standard of conduct more stringent than that of the bad man in Holmes' famous theory of the law—the man who gives heed only to the threat that the public force will be brought to bear against him.[15] The United States has, after all, emphasized the importance of our commitments and the sanctity of our word. Yet the Administration has regarded only lightly our commitment to respect the neutrality and territorial integrity of a small and weak nation and our explicit promises not to conduct military activity on its territory without its consent. We have talked of the evil of violence, yet the Administration has, almost casually, brought the unspeakable violence and destruction and death of modern war to yet another remote and heretofore relatively peaceful land. We speak of law and order. And yet the Administration has ignored what is in my view the essential guiding principle of world law and world order: to confine within the narrowest limits the situations in which we are prepared to condone or legitimate unilateral decisions to resort to force.

I opened with a reference to remarks I had made almost ten years ago as Legal Adviser. With your indulgence I will close with another. In April 1961, a few weeks after the Bay of Pigs, I addressed for the first time the Annual Meeting of the American Society of International Law. I said then:

---

[15] Holmes, Path of the Law, reprinted in J. Marke, The Holmes Reader 41 (2d ed. 1964).

40

A nation which professes to live by the rule of law invites a sure penalty, sometimes more swiftly than by the judgment of a court, if it turns from the path of the law. For us and our associates, moreover, whether we will profess to live by the law is not an issue of policy on which we have alternatives. The answer is inherent in our national tradition, in our culture and it is implicit in the purposes for which we strive in the world. It is implicit in our avowal at birth of "a decent respect for the opinions of mankind." Thus it seems to me we will have a hard time in developing a doctrine as to the use of force which will permit us to be judge in our own case. As in other aspects of our world struggle, the character of our goals and the character of our society impose disadvantages upon us, at least in the short run. This may well appear a harsh and severe doctrine, but then democracy has never been advertised as a simple or an easy way of life.[16]

I think those words can stand now, a few weeks after the Cambodian invasion, as well as they did then, a few weeks after the Bay of Pigs. It was easier for the Legal Adviser to speak those words then, than it would be now, however. For by that time President Kennedy had confessed error and accepted the responsibility.

Confession of error, I am aware, is a harsh prescription. But it should be possible—and without humiliation—for a man who is big enough to be President of the United States.

---

[16] Proceedings of the Am. Soc'y Int'l L., 55th Annual Meeting 205 (1961).

# REBUTTALS

Chairman Carey:

And now I would like to ask each of our principal speakers if he would care to speak further for approximately two minutes. Assistant Attorney General Rehnquist?

Mr. Rehnquist:

I would like to make just one comment where I think I do perhaps differ from Dean McKay and that is with respect to the Korean situation. To me that has stood as the high-water mark of Presidential initiative without prior congressional authorization and it still does. Granted, there was a United Nation's Security Council resolution. However, I have always understood that the law is well established that although a treaty may have the status of a statute it cannot change the constitutional distribution of power between the President and Congress. Therefore since the President's action in Korea was not authorized by Congress nor formally ratified, that action is a rather significant precedent for those who oppose the legality of President Nixon's action. On the consensus issue Korea was in many senses an unpopular war and the constitutional basis of the President's action was debated from the beginning. It was unpopular with the people. It may be that wars in general are unpopular but if that is going to be some sort of constitutional test we had better discuss a lot of other wars besides this one.

Dean McKay:

The question on which Mr. Rehnquist and I differ involves the legality of the present action in Cambodia; and I'll come back to that issue in a moment. But the other question, on which we apparently do not differ, seems to me to be even more important. That is the question whether Congress has the authority to recall the troops, at least in the absence of a confession of error by the President, as Professor Chayes properly recommends.

I do not come to speak for the Cooper-Church bill or the McGovern-Hatfield bill. Rather, it is my purpose to discuss the validity of those proposals; and I see no constitutional difficulty in them. Congress indisputably has the authority to make appropriations, to regulate the land and naval forces, and thus to recall troops, to withdraw appropriations, and to limit appropriations to whatever use is reasonable in the judgment of Congress.

These proposals do not suggest any precipitate withdrawal. If Congress believes that military forces should be withdrawn

42

from Cambodia in the present circumstances, I have no doubt that Congress has the power to require orderly withdrawal.

As to the question on which Mr. Rehnquist and I differ, there is no real doubt in my mind that the President had the *power* to order American military forces into Cambodia. But I do doubt that he had the *authority* to do so. There is, I think, a difference in these circumstances between power and authority. It is here that the unwritten Constitution is of real consequence to us and should be to the President. Unless the President is willing to test out a proposed course of action, at least with congressional leaders, with his cabinet, with principal allies, and conceivably with informed segments of the American public, it seems to me that he has endangered the consensus necessary to the governing of this nation.

Whether that principle was violated in Korea is a question that will always be debated; but at least the situation was quite different there than in Cambodia. President Truman acted abruptly in response to invasion. President Nixon acted abruptly when there was no invasion. President Truman secured approval almost immediately from the Security Council of the United Nations and from Congress. President Nixon has secured no approval.

If Congress should now withdraw any implicit authority that might be inferred from past congressional action, I can see no choice under the Constitution but for the President to remove American military forces from Cambodia.

Mr. Stevenson:

In talking about the conflict between scholars on what happened in Viet Nam before the present Administration took office, I emphasized the fact that in so many instances the problem is one of a dispute as to the facts rather than basic differences as to the law. I think that in this particular situation of Cambodia we have one very great advantage, factually. The President has made certain very definite statements with respect to the limitation on this action and, as the Secretary himself has said in talking to a number of student groups that have come to Washington, all we have to do is wait and see what happens by July 1. The President himself has indicated that he expects the South Vietnamese troops also to get out at approximately the same time. Well let's just wait and see what the facts are.

Now, secondly, to me the most important single issue here is the precedential effect of this action and therefore I am a little bit disturbed about one feature of what Abe Chayes said.

I think that this action should in no way be equated with pre-emptive action, such as the famous case of the British Fleet in 1807 capturing the Danish Fleet at Copenhagen, because of the threat that it would be turned over to the French or, again in Vichy French days, the British action in destroying the French Fleet at Oran. As I demonstrated by numerous figures, in the present situation we very clearly had a continuing armed attack from Cambodia against South Viet Nam and our troops in South Viet Nam. This is clearly a question of armed attack and not of preemptive strike. I think that is a terribly important distinction. In the Cuban missile crisis there was no question of a prior attack on the United States from Cuba. Therefore, it was important in that case—and I quite agree that it was very imaginative, creative legal work—not to use a self-defense argument where there was a mere threat. However, in determining the proportionality of a self-defense action across an international border once there has been an armed attack, certainly one of the questions that you consider is the nature of the threat as well as the continuing armed attack. I do think it is important not to look at this as a precedent for preemptive action.

Mr. Chayes:

I agree that we ought to wait and see until July 1; but I note even today in the front page of the *New York Times* that arrangements apparently are being made between the Lon Nol Government and the South Vietnamese for a continued South Vietnamese presence, and I assume that that will involve United States support in one way or another.

Second, I both sympathize and support Mr. Stevenson's desire to limit the precedential effect of the action here. Although having had a little experience in the same kind of effort, I am not as sure as he is that it will be so easy to do. The whole difference or perhaps the essential difference between us in dealing with the concept of armed attack turns on this question of whether the response was necessary at that time and in advance of resort to international processes established for these purposes. And on that score it does seem to me that the recital of a long history of incursions from the sanctuary really cuts against the government's case rather than for it. It suggests that the moment chosen was not a moment forced upon us by the other side and one to which we had no choice, but a moment chosen at our discretion and, as Secretary Laird said, because suddenly there opened up an opportunity in the change of government in Cambodia to do something that we thought would help us. Now, if I were trying to confine the concept of armed attack as a precedent-making effort, I would try to confine it to those cases where the action was thrust upon us rather than those where we chose the occasion and the means of response with comparative freedom.

# Questions and Statements
# From the Floor

# QUESTIONS AND STATEMENTS FROM THE FLOOR

Chairman Carey:

We have cards from persons wishing the floor and I will take them in ascending order of time requested. The first person has in fact written his question on the back and I will simply read that question. It is from Mr. Melvin S. Hodges: "Why hasn't SEATO been convened 'to agree on measures'? Is the process too cumbersome or is there the likelihood that other signatories will use the occasion to embarrass the United States?"

Mr. Stevenson:

I would like to answer that very briefly. We are not relying on SEATO as justification for the action in Cambodia because we do not regard this as an action of collective self-defense with the Cambodian government but rather a continuation of collective self-defense of South Viet Nam in which we are already engaged.

Chairman Carey:

Mr. Thomas E. Engle has requested the floor for one minute. Mr. Engle, will you please go to this microphone and that way your voice will be taken down by the tape.

Mr. Engle:

I just have two questions for Mr. Rehnquist. One of them is that if the congressional approval of the Gulf of Tonkin Resolution was indicative of what you call the President and Congress acting together and therefore the Government acting in a strong fashion, and that it would be an incentive to agree on the constitutionality of the commitment, then why has the Administration not opposed repeal of the Tonkin Gulf Resolution in Secretary Richardson's letter to Senator Fulbright?

The second question is that I think that the *Curtiss-Wright* case[1] is distinguishable from the Viet Nam situation because there it was the President's foreign relations power which was involved and not the power to go to war which is vested in the Congress. So that although it might be true that the *Curtiss-Wright* case is important, it is because it is an excuse for the Court not to exercise jurisdiction. But I don't think that it solves the constitutionality aspect from the point of view of delegating a power to go to war which, it seems to me, the Gulf of Tonkin Resolution does when it says that the Congress supports actions

---

[1] United States v. Curtiss-Wright Corp., 299 U.S. 304 (1936).

as the President determines. The second operative phrase which you quoted and that phrase as the President determined it, seems to me to delegate that constitutional power away.

Mr. Rehnquist:

As to the reason for the Administration not opposing the repeal of the Gulf of Tonkin Resolution, I think Mr. Stevenson might well be better informed to answer the question than I am. It is my understanding that the Administration feels that there is nothing inconsistent with the position it is taking about winding up hostilities in Viet Nam and the repeal of the Gulf of Tonkin Resolution. The repeal of that resolution obviously doesn't wipe out six years of history or remove whatever number of thousands of troops there are in the field at the time. I would assume that it would be an indication of lack of congressional sanction for further action that could be justified only with the joint approval of the President and Congress. Insofar as your question about the *Curtiss-Wright* case is concerned, I quite agree with you that it is factually distinguishable on the ground that there the Court discussed the foreign affairs power where, as here, we are dealing with the war power. However, I do think that the fact that these powers were treated by Justice Sutherland as being powers dealing with external affairs suggests that, if he had had the same question in connection with the war power, he would have reached the same result. I would just read one paragraph from *Curtiss-Wright:*

> It results that the investment of the federal government with the powers of external sovereignty did not depend upon the affirmative grants of the Constitution. The powers to declare and wage war, to conclude peace, to make treaties, to maintain diplomatic relations with other sovereignties, if they had never been mentioned in the Constitution, would have vested in the federal government as necessary concomitants of nationality.[2]

Since one of the bases of the *Schechter* case was the concept that delegated powers cannot be reallocated,[3] here we have the Supreme Court saying that, in effect, these are not delegated powers in the same way powers over domestic activities are.

Chairman Carey:

Thank you Mr. Rehnquist. Now a one-minute question for you from Amasa Miller.

---

[2] Id. at 318.
[3] Schechter Poultry Corp. v. United States, 295 U.S. 495, 529 (1935).

Mr. Miller:

Mr. Rehnquist, I had a constitutional question which I don't think is really frivolous under your interpretation of the President's powers as to whether or not he deems it necessary to employ a military force of this country in a foreign war. Let's posit that the President had employed those forces in a fashion in which say 50 per cent of the people and 50 per cent of, let's say, at least one of the Houses of Congress where the people's selected representatives sit, not only disapproved of what the President had done in employing those forces but feel it to be a violation of their own principles and of the principles that they believe this country does and should stand for. My question is, what do you believe to be the constitutional right, if any, of such dissenting groups to achieve control of the President's actions and to compel him to cease such employment of American forces?

Mr. Rehnquist:

I suppose there are two remedies available, one is whatever remedy the courts may afford—which is certainly not a large one in the area of international affairs. For the other one I can do little better than to quote Chief Justice Waite in *Munn v. Illinois*[4] that your resort in some cases has to be to the polls rather than to the courts.

Mr. Miller:

May I respond to that just momentarily? I am assuming the situation here in which a resort to the polls some two years later with the question of whether engaging in military activity would violate the principles of 50 per cent of the people and 50 per cent of their representatives would not be very satisfactory in human terms; do you think so? That is the reason I based my question on constitutional grounds—not to persuade or not to try to get something different than what is the constitutional right, if any, to achieve control, to regain control, of what this country is doing with its military forces under those circumstances.

Mr. Rehnquist:

Mr. Miller, to extend your question departs from a strict constitutional interpretation by taking into effect what these people can do. I mean, I dare say, this is not the first time in the nation's history that a number of people, of whatever percentage I do not know, want the President to do something different than he has done and I think in the past . . . .

---

4 94 U.S. 113, 134 (1877).

Mr. Miller:

Are you ignoring my assumption, which is that 50 per cent of the people feel that this is a violation of their principles and the principles they believe the country should stand for? Are you ignoring that?

Mr. Rehnquist:
Not at all.

Mr. Miller:
And you would still give the same answer?

Mr. Rehnquist:
Precisely.

Mr. Miller:
Well, I think that's quite amazing.

Chairman Carey:
Now, Professors Friedmann, Gardner and Henkin wish to read statements of their own.

Mr. Wolfgang Friedmann:*
I should like to speak very briefly to the international law aspects of the matter. It seems to me that unless we consider the question on at least three different levels we are apt to lose sight of the woods for the trees. The first level is that of an isolated incident in response to a violation of neutrality. If you take it in that way, as Mr. Stevenson suggested, it is still arguable that this was not a *Caroline* situation of responding to an overwhelming and instant necessity (*i.e.*, an imminent attack). Indeed the American troops had great difficulty in finding the Vietnamese when they crossed the frontier. But then this is not a situation like say American bombers or troops responding to hostile action in the form of either an actual or imminent attack from full placements opposite their own frontiers. There would not be anything like the outcry there has been if this had been merely an isolated incident in response to a violation of neutrality or even an *Altmark* situation. Whether the British action in entering a Norwegian fjord in 1940 to liberate captured British seamen from a prison ship was legal, is doubtful.[5] In any case, it differed in several important respects from the Cambodia situation.

---

* Professor of International Law, Columbia University.
[5] Borchard, Was Norway Delinquent in the Case of the Altmark?, 34 Am. J. Int'l L. 289 (1940).

Second, I come to Mr. Stevenson's argument that we should not bring in the Viet Nam situation, although later he seemed to mean that he rested his case entirely on the rights or wrongs of the Viet Nam situation. Only if the United States position is one of legitimate individual or collective self-defense under article 51, could the Cambodia action be justified. Now we cannot go again into the Viet Nam argument but I think it is essential to stress that the Cambodian issue stands and falls together with the Viet Nam argument; those of us who have never been able to regard the United States posture in Viet Nam as a response to an aggression in self-defense, individual or collective, but as a deliberate action taken since 1954 to build up an anti-communist bastion and to prevent elections which under the Geneva Accords were to be held in 1956, cannot regard this new extension as an article 51 posture.

The third, and most important point—one touched upon by Professor Chayes—goes I think to the cause of the quite unprecedented commotion this action has caused far beyond the Viet Nam situation. It is important that the United States did not bother to seek the consent of the wobbling Cambodian Government—as it did in the Dominican situation. In fact, the United States is acting more and more like its major opponents; it is more and more disdainful of the integrity of small nations which it professes to respect inside or outside the United Nations Charter. It acts like an imperial power controlling a region. Mr. Stevenson said, sincerely but I think wrongly, that this was not a war against the Cambodian people. As in Viet Nam, the principal consequence of this involvement which is now spreading war over the continent—whether or not the people agree—is that of involving more and more millions in death, destruction and dislocation. In the wider context of international law it means that the United States can no longer pretend to be a champion of independence and self-determination of nations; and this is indeed a very serious matter.

Mr. Richard Gardner:*
While I have serious reservations about our action in Cambodia from the point of view of policy, I think the question of its legality under international law is a closely balanced one. First, let me define what I mean when I ask the question: "Is our action in Cambodia legal?" I mean is it an action which can be justified under generally accepted principles of inter-

* Henry L. Moses Professor of Law and International Organization, Columbia University.

national law which we are prepared to live with in the future, and which we are going to ask others to live with in the future. Obviously we cannot claim a freedom to act in one case which we are not prepared to grant to others in another case. The Cambodian action presents great difficulties for legal analysis because there are few relevant historical precedents to guide us and because the facts are in dispute—even among the members of this panel.

It seems to me that there are three issues. The first issue is whether there is consent on the part of the Cambodian Government—such consent as which would legitimize the action of the United States and South Viet Nam. Mr. Chayes expressed surprise at some of the statements made by Mr. Stevenson which emphasized the subsequent manifestation of consent. I do not know why he should have been surprised. The Department of State issued some days ago a paper which said, and I would like to quote it because this is the most complete statement on the record at this point:

> The Cambodians could not ask for help from American forces because to do so would be a renunciation of neutrality, and in effect would join them and South Viet-Nam and its allies against North Viet-Nam. Initially, Prime Minister Lon Nol said that no foreign troops would be required; that only additional arms and equipment would be needed for Cambodia's defense. When this proved insufficient, he appealed for assistance of ethnic Cambodians serving with the South Vietnamese army forces.
>
> While Prime Minister Lon Nol was not asked to approve or agree in advance to the joint military operations against the sanctuaries, he has said that this action represents a positive U.S. response to Cambodia's appeal for help in restoring its neutrality and repelling North Vietnamese and Viet Cong invaders.[6]

To sum up on this first point, I think we have a complex factual and legal issue as to whether we can regard the United States action as legal on the basis of consent, on the theory that it was a response to a general appeal for help which the Cambodian government has subsequently described as a justified response.

The second issue is whether this is a justified act of self-defense under Article 51 of the United Nations Charter, which of course does require an armed attack. Mr. Stevenson emphasises that in the Government's view there was a continuing armed attack from the Cambodian sanctuaries into South Viet Nam and thus a self-defense justification was available to both

---

[6] Department of State, Bureau of Public Affairs, Questions and Answers—The Situation in Cambodia 3-4 (May 1970).

ourselves and the South Vietnamese. If I understand Mr. Chayes, his objection is—why at this moment? Why, after four years, do we claim a right of self-defense now? Here again we have a factual problem. The Government's argument again is set up in detail in this State Department document which I commend to Mr. Chayes:

> In April the North Vietnamese began moving more actively out of their sanctuaries and deeper into Cambodia in an effort to establish a solid Communist-held zone reaching to Sihanoukville and the sea along 600 miles of the Cambodian-South Vietnamese border. This would have given them a far stronger position in Cambodia than they ever had; it would have assured them of potentially unlimited supply and replacement capabilities; and it would thus have posed a critically increased threat to remaining U.S. forces nearby across the South Vietnamese border.[7]

The document concludes: "The problem presented to President Nixon in late April was thus wholly different, both politically and militarily, than the situation which existed previously."[8] Frankly, I do not believe any of us here command the facts which can either confirm or deny these factual claims. We are dependent on our government and its recital of the facts and the question is whether we want to stipulate them as true or not.

The third issue is whether, apart from article 51, there is some other legal justification for our action in Cambodia—whether we apply the old *Caroline* doctrine of preemptive self-defense without an armed attack or whether we make an argument based upon the *Altmark* case and other cases. I am very uncertain about this because I think it is an open question whether a belligerent has the right to take limited acts on neutral territory for the sole purpose of bringing to an end acts by another belligerent on that territory which are threatening it and its allies. On its face, and in the light of *Altmark*, that is not such an unreasonable proposition. It needs further analysis.

On two things, however, I do have firm views. One is that the Government should have gone to the Security Council immediately because I believe the doctrine of exhaustion of remedies is a very important one in both international and in domestic law. Article 37 of the United Nations Charter says that parties to a dispute which may threaten international peace *shall* refer to the Security Council. I think the United States should have gone to the council even if we were convinced it would yield no result. I think our whole posture domestically and

---

[7] Id. at 1.
[8] Id. at 4.

53

internationally would be improved. The second thing I am clear on is that, with great respect to our distinguished Legal Adviser, it is most unfortunate that his office did not issue promptly a brief giving the legal basis of our action in Cambodia. It is also most unfortunate that the President's statement on Cambodia made no reference to the United Nations Charter or other sources of international law. We should always be willing to state the legal basis of our action lest we give the impression that we regard ourselves as above the law.

My last point is a general one. I am very deeply concerned at what I regard as the increasing tendency in our country, and even in our law schools, to subordinate law to politics. I am against the Viet Nam war, but I do not regard our presence in Viet Nam as illegal. I believe we must discuss the political and legal issues separately. We must also take care not to take legal positions because they serve our political objectives at the moment.

Mr. Louis Henkin:*

I intervene principally because I am somewhat worried about the trend of this debate. Those of us who are shocked by the Cambodian action have been tempted to attack it with constitutional and other legal arguments which we might be reluctant to make in other contexts. I believe President Nixon's action was outrageous, but not everything that is outrageous is illegal, and I should not wish to distort the relevant constitutional or international law that governs our future.

One source of distortion is that we have attempted to discuss Cambodia virtually in isolation from Viet Nam, probably because Viet Nam itself has been debated "dry." But one cannot deal with Cambodia as though it were a new and separate war, whether for constitutional purposes or under international law.

I am particularly concerned about the constitutional debates. In my view President Nixon required authorization from Congress to engage in this war in Viet Nam-Cambodia and in my view he has had that authorization.[9] I have no doubt that Congress can cancel or withdraw its authorization. But if Congress will not do it, the answer is not to conjure up constitutional limitations on the President's power. That would be foolish, perhaps disastrous. We cannot afford to deal with Presidential

---

* Professor of International Law, Columbia University.
[9] See, e.g., Henkin, Constitutional Issues in Foreign Policy, 23 J. of Int'l Affairs 210 (1969).

errror by curtailing Presidential power. We have to elect better Presidents.

The discussion of the international legality of the Cambodian action is troublesome in another way. Again, some of the arguments being made to condemn President Nixon's incursion into Cambodia are not arguments we would make in other contexts. I do not know whether the Cambodian Government consented or acquiesced, but it is far from obvious that United States troops entered or remain against the wishes of that Government, and I would hardly build a case on that proposition. Suggestions that subsequent consent or ratification cannot be effective are difficult to accept. (I remind my friend Professor Chayes of his own discussion of "Authorization by the Security Council" under Article 53 of the United Nations Charter in the case of the Cuban missile crisis and our Dominican intervention.)[10] Nor would I wish to argue that a state cannot act in self-defense against an armed attack by troops of one state operating on the territory of another; I wonder what those who are tempted to doubt that right would say about the actions of the State of Israel against guerrilla attacks from Lebanese soil.

In general I think the Cambodian action changes very little the legal issues of the Viet Nam war. As to them, as Mr. Stevenson has said, much depends on one's view of the facts, perhaps even more on how one characterizes them. For the lawyer much turns on whether one sees a civil war in South Viet Nam, with intervention by North Viet Nam and the United States; or a civil war between North and South Viet Nam, with intervention by the United States; or—as the official United States position now has it—an armed attack by North Viet Nam against South Viet Nam with the United States acting in defense of South Viet Nam under Article 51 of the Charter. Of course, it may be that there are all three of these wars going on at the same time and if so United States intervention in one of them is probably illegal under traditional international law if not under the Charter.

Finally, I wish to echo at least one of the views of Professor Chayes and my colleague Professor Friedmann. Even if one cannot convict the United States of any new violation of international law by its Cambodian excursion, the Administration has hardly shown particular concern for international law.

---

[10] See Chayes, Law and the Quarantine of Cuba, 41 Foreign Affairs 550, 555-57 (1963), reprinted in part in 2 A. Chayes, T. Ehrlich & A. Lowenfeld, International Legal Process 1091-92 (1968).

# Documentary Supplement

# THE CONSTITUTION OF THE UNITED STATES

. . . .

## ARTICLE I

. . . .

SECTION 8. The Congress shall have Power To lay and collect Taxes, Duties, Imposts and Excises, to pay the Debts and provide for the common Defence and general Welfare of the United States . . . .

. . . .

To declare War, grant Letters of Marque and Reprisal, and make Rules concerning Captures on Land and Water;

To raise and support Armies, but no Appropriation of Money to that Use shall be for a longer Term than two Years;

To provide and maintain a Navy;

To make Rules for the Government and Regulation of the land and naval Forces;

. . . .

To make all Laws which shall be necessary and proper for carrying into Execution the foregoing Powers, and all other Powers vested by this Constitution in the Government of the United States, or in any Department or Officer thereof.

. . . .

## ARTICLE II

SECTION 1. The executive Power shall be vested in a President of the United States of America.

. . . .

SECTION 2. The President shall be Commander in Chief of the Army and Navy of the United States, . . . .

He shall have Power, by and with the Advice and Consent of the Senate, to make Treaties, provided two thirds of the Senators present concur; . . . .

. . . .

SECTION 3. . . . . he shall take Care that the Laws be faithfully executed, and shall Commission all the Officers of the United States.

. . . .

# CHARTER OF THE UNITED NATIONS

As amended to December 31, 1969

. . . .

## CHAPTER I

### PURPOSES AND PRINCIPLES

### ARTICLE 1

The Purposes of the United Nations are:

1. To maintain international peace and security, and to that end: to take effective collective measures for the prevention and removal of threats to the peace, and for the suppression of acts of aggression or other breaches of the peace, and to bring about by peaceful means, and in conformity with the principles of justice and international law, adjustment or settlement of international disputes or situations which might lead to a breach of the peace;

. . . .

### ARTICLE 2

The Organization and its Members, in pursuit of the Purposes stated in Article 1, shall act in accordance with the following Principles.

1. The Organization is based on the principle of the sovereign equality of all its Members.

2. All Members, in order to ensure to all of them the rights and benefits resulting from membership, shall fulfil in good faith the obligations assumed by them in accordance with the present Charter.

3. All Members shall settle their international disputes by peaceful means in such a manner that international peace and security, and justice, are not endangered.

4. All Members shall refrain in their international relations from the threat or use of force against the territorial integrity or political independence of any state, or in any other manner inconsistent with the Purposes of the United Nations.

5. All Members shall give the United Nations every assistance in any action it takes in accordance with the present Charter, and shall refrain from giving assistance to any state against which the United Nations is taking preventive or enforcement action.

6. The Organization shall ensure that states which are not Members of the United Nations act in accordance with these

58

Principles so far as may be necessary for the maintenance of international peace and security.

7. Nothing contained in the present Charter shall authorize the United Nations to intervene in matters which are essentially within the domestic jurisdiction of any state or shall require the Members to submit such matters to settlement under the present Charter; but this principle shall not prejudice the application of enforcement measures under Chapter VII.

. . . .

# CHAPTER VI
## PACIFIC SETTLEMENT OF DISPUTES
### ARTICLE 33

1. The parties to any dispute, the continuance of which is likely to endanger the maintenance of international peace and security, shall, first of all, seek a solution by negotiation, enquiry, mediation, conciliation, arbitration, judicial settlement, resort to regional agencies or arrangements, or other peaceful means of their own choice.

2. The Security Council shall, when it deems necessary, call upon the parties to settle their dispute by such means.

. . . .

### ARTICLE 36

1. The Security Council may, at any stage of a dispute of the nature referred to in Article 33 or of a situation of like nature, recommend appropriate procedures or methods of adjustment.

2. The Security Council should take into consideration any procedures for the settlement of the dispute which have already been adopted by the parties.

. . . .

### ARTICLE 37

1. Should the parties to a dispute of the nature referred to in Article 33 fail to settle it by the means indicated in that Article, they shall refer it to the Security Council.

2. If the Security Council deems that the continuance of the dispute is in fact likely to endanger the maintenance of international peace and security, it shall decide whether to take action under Article 36 or to recommend such terms of settlement as it may consider appropriate.

. . . .

# ARTICLE 51

Nothing in the present Charter shall impair the inherent right of individual or collective self-defence if an armed attack occurs against a Member of the United Nations, until the Security Council has taken measures necessary to maintain international peace and security. Measures taken by Members in the exercise of this right of self-defence shall be immediately reported to the Security Council and shall not in any way affect the authority and responsibility of the Security Council under the present Charter to take at any time such action as it deems necessary in order to maintain or restore international peace and security.

# AGREEMENT OF THE CESSATION OF HOSTILITIES IN CAMBODIA, JULY 20, 1954[1]

## CHAPTER I—PRINCIPLES AND CONDITIONS GOVERNING EXECUTION OF THE CEASE-FIRE

### Article 1

As from twenty-third July 1954 at 0800 hours (Peking mean time) complete cessation of all hostilities throughout Cambodia shall be ordered and enforced by the Commanders of the Armed Forces of the two parties for all troops and personnel of the land, naval and air forces under their control.

. . . .

### Article 6

The situation of these nationals shall be decided in the light of the Declaration made by the Delegation of Cambodia at the Geneva Conference, reading as follows:

"The Royal Government of Cambodia,

In the desire to ensure harmony and agreement among the peoples of the Kingdom,

Declares itself resolved to take the necessary measures to integrate all citizens, without discrimination, into the national community and to guarantee them the enjoyment of the rights and freedoms for which the Constitution of the Kingdom provides;

Affirms that all Cambodian citizens may freely participate as electors or candidates in general elections by secret ballot."

No reprisals shall be taken against the said nationals or their families, each national being entitled to the enjoyment, without any discrimination as compared with other nationals, of all constitutional guarantees concerning the protection of person and property and democratic freedoms.

Applicants therefor may be accepted for service in the Regular Army or local police formations if they satisfy the conditions required for current recruitment of the Army and Police Corps.

The same procedure shall apply to those persons who have returned to civilian life and who may apply for civilian employment on the same terms as other nationals.

---

[1] IC/52, 21 July 1954, Original: French.

## B. BAN ON THE INTRODUCTION OF FRESH TROOPS, MILITARY PERSONNEL, ARMAMENTS AND MUNITIONS, MILITARY BASES

*Article 7*

In accordance with the Declaration made by the Delegation of Cambodia at 2400 hours on 20 July 1954 at the Geneva Conference of Foreign Ministers:

"The Royal Government of Cambodia will not join in any agreement with other States, if this agreement carries for Cambodia the obligation to enter into a military alliance not in conformity with the principles of the Charter of the United Nations, or, as long as its security is not threatened, the obligation to establish bases on Cambodian territory for the military forces of foreign powers.

"During the period which will elapse between the date of the cessation of hostilities in Viet-Nam and that of the final settlement of political problems in this country, the Royal Government of Cambodia will not solicit foreign aid in war materiel, personnel or instructors except for the purpose of the effective defence of the territory."

# FINAL DECLARATION OF GENEVA CONFERENCE, JULY 21, 1954[1]

Final declaration, dated July 21, 1954, of the Geneva Conference on the problem of restoring peace in Indo-China, in which the representatives of Cambodia, the Democratic Republic of Viet-Nam, France, Laos, the People's Republic of China, the State of Viet-Nam, the Union of Soviet Socialist Republics, the United Kingdom, and the United States of America took part.

1. The Conference takes note of the agreements ending hostilities in Cambodia, Laos and Viet-Nam and organizing international control and the supervision of the execution of the provisions of these agreements.

2. The Conference expresses satisfaction at the ending of hostilities in Cambodia, Laos and Viet-Nam; the Conference expresses its conviction that the execution of the provisions set out in the present declaration and in the agreements on the cessation of hostilities will permit Cambodia, Laos and Viet-Nam henceforth to play their part, in full independence and sovereignty, in the peaceful community of nations.

3. The Conference takes note of the declarations made by the Governments of Cambodia and of Laos of their intention to adopt measures permitting all citizens to take their place in the national community, in particular by participating in the next general elections, which, in conformity with the constitution of each of these countries, shall take place in the course of the year 1955, by secret ballot and in conditions of respect for fundamental freedoms.

4. The Conference takes note of the clauses in the agreement on the cessation of hostilities in Viet-Nam prohibiting the introduction into Viet-Nam of foreign troops and military personnel as well as of all kinds of arms and munitions. The Conference also takes note of the declarations made by the Governments of Cambodia and Laos of their resolution not to request foreign aid, whether in war material, in personnel or in instructors except for the purpose of the effective defence of their territory and, in the case of Laos, to the extent defined by the agreements on the cessation of hostilities in Laos.

5. The Conference takes note of the clauses in the agreement on the cessation of hostilities in Viet-Nam to the effect that no military base under the control of a foreign State may be established in the regrouping zones of the two parties, the latter

---

[1] 31 Dep't State Bull. 164 (1954).

having the obligation to see that the zones allotted to them shall not constitute part of any military alliance and shall not be utilized for the resumption of hostilities or in the service of an aggressive policy. The Conference also takes note of the declarations of the Governments of Cambodia and Laos to the effect that they will not join in any agreement with other States if this agreement includes the obligation to participate in a military alliance not in conformity with the principles of the Charter of the United Nations or, in the case of Laos, with the principles of the agreement on the cessation of hostilities in Laos or, so long as their security is not threatened, the obligation to establish bases on Cambodian or Laotian territory for the military forces of foreign Powers.

6. The Conference recognizes that the essential purpose of the agreement relating to Viet-Nam is to settle military questions with a view to ending hostilities and that the military demarcation line is provisional and should not in any way be interpreted as constituting a political or territorial boundary. The Conference expresses its conviction that the execution of the provisions set out in the present declaration and in the agreement on the cessation of hostilities creates the necessary basis for the achievement in the near future of a political settlement in Viet-Nam.

7. The Conference declares that, so far as Viet-Nam is concerned, the settlement of political problems, effected on the basis of respect for the principles of independence, unity and territorial integrity, shall permit the Vietnamese people to enjoy the fundamental freedoms, guaranteed by democratic institutions established as a result of free general elections by secret ballot. In order to ensure that sufficient progress in the restoration of peace has been made, and that all the necessary conditions obtain for free expression of the national will, general elections shall be held in July 1956, under the supervision of an international commission composed of representatives of the Member States of the International Supervisory Commission, referred to in the agreement on the cessation of hostilities. Consultations will be held on this subject between the competent representative authorities of the two zones from 20 July 1955 onwards.

8. The provisions of the agreements on the cessation of hostilities intended to ensure the protection of individuals and of property must be most strictly applied and must, in particular, allow everyone in Viet-Nam to decide freely in which zone he wishes to live.

9. The competent representative authorities of the Northern

and Southern zones of Viet-Nam, as well as the authorities of Laos and Cambodia, must not permit any individual or collective reprisals against persons who have collaborated in any way with one of the parties during the war, or against members of such persons' families.

. . . .

12. In their relations with Cambodia, Laos and Viet-Nam, each member of the Geneva Conference undertakes to respect the sovereignty, the independence, the unity and the territorial integrity of the above-mentioned states, and to refrain from any interference in their internal affairs.

13. The members of the Conference agree to consult one another on any question which may be referred to them by the International Supervisory Commission in order to study such measures as may prove necessary to ensure that the agreements on the cessation of hostilities in Cambodia, Laos and Viet-Nam are respected.

## THE CEASE-FIRE AGREEMENTS IN INDOCHINA:
### Statement by the President, July 21, 1954[1]

I am glad, of course, that agreement has been reached at Geneva to stop the bloodshed in Indochina.

The United States has not been a belligerent in the war. The primary responsibility for the settlement in Indochina rested with those nations which participated in the fighting. Our role at Geneva has been at all times to try to be helpful where desired and to aid France and Cambodia, Laos, and Viet-Nam to obtain a just and honorable settlement which will take into account the needs of the interested people. Accordingly, the United States has not itself been party to or bound by the decisions taken by the Conference, but it is our hope that it will lead to the establishment of peace consistent with the rights and the needs of the countries concerned. The agreement contains features which we do not like, but a great deal depends on how they work in practice.

The United States is issuing at Geneva a statement to the effect that it is not prepared to join in the Conference declaration, but, as loyal members of the United Nations, we also say that, in compliance with the obligations and principles contained in article 2 of the United Nations Charter, the United States will not use force to disturb the settlement. We also say that any renewal of Communist aggression would be viewed by us as a matter of grave concern.

As evidence of our resolve to assist Cambodia and Laos to play their part, in full independence and sovereignty, in the peaceful community of free nations, we are requesting the agreement of the Governments of Cambodia and Laos to our appointment of an Ambassador or Minister to be resident at their respective capitals (Phnom Penh and Vientiane). We already have a Chief of Mission at Saigon, the Capital of Viet-Nam, and this Embassy will, of course, be maintained.

The United States is actively pursuing discussions with other free nations with a view to the rapid organization of a collective defense in Southeast Asia in order to prevent further direct or indirect Communist aggression in that general area.

[1] 31 Dep't State Bull. 163 (1954).

## STATEMENT BY THE UNDER SECRETARY OF STATE[1]
## AT THE CONCLUDING PLENARY SESSION
## OF THE GENEVA CONFERENCE,
## JULY 21, 1954[2]

As I stated on July 18, my Government is not prepared to join in a declaration by the Conference such as is submitted. However, the United States makes this unilateral declaration of its position in these matters:

*Declaration*

The Government of the United States being resolved to devote its efforts to the strengthening of peace in accordance with the principles and purposes of the United Nations takes note of the agreements concluded at Geneva on July 20 and 21, 1954 between (a) the Franco-Laotian Command and the Command of the Peoples Army of Viet-Nam; (b) the Royal Khmer Army Command and the Command of the Peoples Army of Viet-Nam; (c) Franco-Vietnamese Command and the Command of the Peoples Army of Viet-Nam and of paragraphs 1 to 12 inclusive of the declaration presented to the Geneva Conference on July 21, 1954 declares with regard to the aforesaid agreements and paragraphs that (i) it will refrain from the threat or the use of force to disturb them, in accordance with Article 2(4) of the Charter of the United Nations dealing with the obligation of members to refrain in their international relations from the threat or use of force; and (ii) it would view any renewal of the aggression in violation of the aforesaid agreements with grave concern and as seriously threatening international peace and security.

In connection with the statement in the declaration concerning free elections in Viet-Nam my Government wishes to make clear its position which it has expressed in a declaration made in Washington on June 29, 1954, as follows:

> In the case of nations now divided against their will, we shall continue to seek to achieve unity through free elections supervised by the United Nations to insure that they are conducted fairly.

With respect to the statement made by the representative of the State of Viet-Nam, the United States reiterates its traditional position that peoples are entitled to determine their own future and that it will not join in an arrangement which would hinder this. Nothing in its declaration just made is intended to or does indicate any departure from this traditional position.

---

[1] Walter Bedell Smith.
[2] 31 Dep't State Bull. 162-63 (1954).

We share the hope that the agreements will permit Cambodia, Laos and Viet-Nam to play their part, in full independence and sovereignty, in the peaceful community of nations, and will enable the peoples of that area to determine their own future.

## SOUTHEAST ASIA COLLECTIVE DEFENSE TREATY AND PROTOCOL THERETO, SEPTEMBER 8, 1954[1]

### Text of Treaty

The Parties to this Treaty,

Recognizing the sovereign equality of all the Parties,

Reiterating their faith in the purposes and principles set forth in the Charter of the United Nations and their desire to live in peace with all peoples and all governments,

Reaffirming that, in accordance with the Charter of the United Nations, they uphold the principle of equal rights and self-determination of peoples, and declaring that they will earnestly strive by every peaceful means to promote self-government and to secure the independence of all countries whose peoples desire it and are able to undertake its responsibilities,

Desiring to strengthen the fabric of peace and freedom and to uphold the principles of democracy, individual liberty and the rule of law, and to promote the economic well-being and development of all peoples in the treaty area,

Intending to declare publicly and formally their sense of unity, so that any potential aggressor will appreciate that the Parties stand together in the area, and

Desiring further to coordinate their efforts for collective defense for the preservation of peace and security,

Therefore agree as follows:

### ARTICLE I

The Parties undertake, as set forth in the Charter of the United Nations, to settle any international disputes in which they may be involved by peaceful means in such a manner that international peace and security and justice are not endangered, and to refrain in their international relations from the threat or use of force in any manner inconsistent with the purposes of the United Nations.

### ARTICLE II

In order more effectively to achieve the objectives of this Treaty the Parties, separately and jointly, by means of continuous and effective self-help and mutual aid will maintain and develop their individual and collective capacity to resist armed attack and to prevent and counter subversive activities directed from without against their territorial integrity and political stability.

---

1 [1955] 6 U.S.T. 81, T.I.A.S. No. 3170, 209 U.N.T.S. 28.

## ARTICLE III

The Parties undertake to strengthen their free institutions and to cooperate with one another in the further development of economic measures, including technical assistance, designed both to promote economic progress and social well-being and to further the individual and collective efforts of governments toward these ends.

## ARTICLE IV

1. Each Party recognizes that aggression by means of armed attack in the treaty area against any of the Parties or against any State or territory which the Parties by unanimous agreement may hereafter designate, would endanger its own peace and safety, and agrees that it will in that event act to meet the common danger in accordance with its constitutional processes. Measures taken under this paragraph shall be immediately reported to the Security Council of the United Nations.

2. If, in the opinion of any of the Parties, the inviolability or the integrity of the territory or the sovereignty or political independence of any Party in the treaty area or of any other State or territory to which the provisions of paragraph 1 of this Article from time to time apply is threatened in any way other than by armed attack or is affected or threatened by any fact or situation which might endanger the peace of the area, the Parties shall consult immediately in order to agree on the measures which should be taken for the common defense.

3. It is understood that no action on the territory of any State designated by unanimous agreement under paragraph 1 of this Article or on any territory so designated shall be taken except at the invitation or with the consent of the government concerned.

## ARTICLE V

The Parties hereby establish a Council, on which each of them shall be represented, to consider matters concerning the implementation of this Treaty. The Council shall provide for consultation with regard to military and any other planning as the situation obtaining in the treaty area may from time to time require. The Council shall be so organized as to be able to meet at any time.

## ARTICLE VI

This Treaty does not affect and shall not be interpreted as affecting in any way the rights and obligations of any of the

Parties under the Charter of the United Nations or the responsibility of the United Nations for the maintenance of international peace and security. Each Party declares that none of the international engagements now in force between it and any other of the Parties or any third party is in conflict with the provisions of this Treaty, and undertakes not to enter into any international engagements in conflict with this Treaty.

## ARTICLE VII

Any other State in a position to further the objectives of this Treaty and to contribute to the security of the area may, by unanimous agreement of the Parties, be invited to accede to this Treaty. Any State so invited may become a Party to the Treaty by depositing its instrument of accession with the Government of the Republic of the Philippines. The Government of the Republic of the Philippines shall inform each of the Parties of the deposit of each such instrument of accession.

## ARTICLE VIII

As used in this Treaty, the "treaty area" is the general area of Southeast Asia, including also the entire territories of the Asian Parties, and the general area of the Southwest Pacific not including the Pacific area north of 21 degrees 30 minutes north latitude. The Parties may, by unanimous agreement, amend this Article to include within the treaty area the territory of any State acceding to this Treaty in accordance with Article VII or otherwise to change the treaty area.

## ARTICLE IX

1. This Treaty shall be deposited in the archives of the Government of the Republic of the Philippines. Duly certified copies thereof shall be transmitted by that government to the other signatories.

2. The Treaty shall be ratified and its provisions carried out by the Parties in accordance with their respective constitutional processes. The instruments of ratification shall be deposited as soon as possible with the Government of the Republic of the Philippines, which shall notify all of the other signatories of such deposit.

3. The Treaty shall enter into force between the States which have ratified it as soon as the instruments of ratification of a majority of the signatories shall have been deposited, and shall come into effect with respect to each other State on the date of the deposit of its instrument of ratification.

# ARTICLE X

This Treaty shall remain in force indefinitely, but any Party may cease to be a Party one year after its notice of denunciation has been given to the Government of the Republic of the Philippines, which shall inform the Governments of the other Parties of the deposit of each notice of denunciation.

# ARTICLE XI

The English text of this Treaty is binding on the Parties, but when the Parties have agreed to the French text thereof and have so notified the Government of the Republic of the Philippines, the French text shall be equally authentic and binding on the Parties.

## Understanding of the United States of America

The United States of America in executing the present Treaty does so with the understanding that its recognition of the effect of aggression and armed attack and its agreement with reference thereto in Article IV, paragraph 1, apply only to communist aggression but affirms that in the event of other aggression or armed attack it will consult under the provisions of Article IV, paragraph 2.

Australia
France
New Zealand
Pakistan: Signed for transmission to my Government for its consideration and action in accordance with the Constitution of Pakistan.
Republic of the Philippines
Kingdom of Thailand
United Kingdom
United States of America

# GULF OF TONKIN RESOLUTION[1]

Whereas naval units of the Communist regime in Vietnam, in violation of the principles of the Charter of the United Nations and of international law, have deliberately and repeatedly attacked United States naval vessels lawfully present in international waters, and have thereby created a serious threat to international peace; and

Whereas these attacks are part of a deliberate and systematic campaign of aggression that the Communist regime in North Viet Nam has been waging against its neighbors and the nations joined with them in the collective defense of their freedom; and

Whereas the United States is assisting the peoples of southeast Asia to protect their freedom and has no territorial, military or political ambitions in that area, but desires only that these peoples should be left in peace to work out their own destinies in their own way: Now, therefore, be it

*Resolved by the Senate and House of Representatives of the United States of America in Congress assembled,* That the Congress approves and supports the determination of the President, as Commander in Chief, to take all necessary measures to repel any armed attack against the forces of the United States and to prevent further aggression.

SEC. 2. The United States regards as vital to its national interest and to world peace the maintenance of international peace and security in southeast Asia. Consonant with the Constitution of the United States and the Charter of the United Nations and in accordance with its obligations under the Southeast Asia Collective Defense Treaty, the United States is, therefore, prepared, as the President determines, to take all necessary steps, including the use of armed force, to assist any member or protocol state of the Southeast Asia Collective Defense Treaty requesting assistance in defense of its freedom.

SEC. 3. This resolution shall expire when the President shall determine that the peace and security of the area is reasonably assured by international conditions created by action of the United Nations or otherwise, except that it may be terminated earlier by concurrent resolution of the Congress.

---

[1] Public Law 88-408 [H.J. Res. 1145], 78 Stat. 384, approved Aug. 10, 1964.

# PRESIDENT'S ADDRESS TO THE NATION: THE SITUATION IN SOUTHEAST ASIA, APRIL 30, 1970.[1]

After full consultation with the National Security Council, Ambassador Bunker, General Abrams, and my other advisers, I have concluded that the actions of the enemy in the last 10 days clearly endanger the lives of Americans who are in Vietnam now and would constitute an unacceptable risk to those who will be there after withdrawal of another 150,000.

To protect our men who are in Vietnam and to guarantee the continued success of our withdrawal and Vietnamization programs, I have concluded that the time has come for action.

. . . .

Cambodia, a small country of 7 million people, has been a neutral nation since the Geneva Agreement of 1954—an agreement, incidentally, which was signed by the Government of North Vietnam.

American policy since then has been to scrupulously respect the neutrality of the Cambodian people. We have maintained a skeleton diplomatic mission of fewer than 15 in Cambodia's capital, and that only since last August. For the previous 4 years, from 1965 to 1969, we did not have any diplomatic mission whatever in Cambodia. And for the past 5 years, we have provided no military assistance whatever and no economic assistance to Cambodia.

North Vietnam, however, has not respected that neutrality.

For the past 5 years—as indicated on this map that you see here—North Vietnam has occupied military sanctuaries all along the Cambodian frontier with South Vietnam. Some of these extend up to 20 miles into Cambodia. . . . They are used for hit and run attacks on American and South Vietnamese forces in South Vietnam.

These Communist occupied territories contain major base camps, training sites, logistics facilities, weapons and ammunition factories, air strips, and prisoner-of-war compounds.

For 5 years, neither the United States nor South Vietnam has moved against these enemy sanctuaries because we did not wish to violate the territory of a neutral nation. Even after the Vietnamese Communists began to expand these sanctuaries 4 weeks ago, we counseled patience to our South Vietnamese allies and imposed restraints on our own commanders.

. . . .

---

[1] 6 Weekly Compilation of Pres'l Doc. 596-601 (May 4, 1970).

In contrast to our policy, the enemy in the past 2 weeks has stepped up his guerrilla actions and he is concentrating his main forces in these sanctuaries that you see on this map where they are building up to launch massive attacks on our forces and those of South Vietnam.

North Vietnam in the last 2 weeks has stripped away all pretense of respecting the sovereignty or the neutrality of Cambodia. Thousands of their soldiers are invading the country from the sanctuaries; they are encircling the capital of Phnom Penh. Coming from these sanctuaries, as you see here, they have moved into Cambodia and are encircling the capital.

Cambodia, as a result of this, has sent out a call to the United States, to a number of other nations, for assistance. Because if this enemy effort succeeds, Cambodia would become a vast enemy staging area and a springboard for attacks on South Vietnam along 600 miles of frontier—a refuge where enemy troops could return from combat without fear of retaliation.

North Vietnamese men and supplies could then be poured into that country, jeopardizing not only the lives of our men but the people of South Vietnam as well.

. . . .

This is not an invasion of Cambodia. The areas in which these attacks will be launched are completely occupied and controlled by North Vietnamese forces. Our purpose is not to occupy the areas. Once enemy forces are driven out of these sanctuaries and once their military supplies are destroyed we will withdraw.

These actions are in no way directed at the security interests of any nation. Any government that chooses to use these actions as a pretext for harming relations with the United States will be doing so on its own responsibility, and on its own initiative, and we will draw the appropriate conclusions.

. . . .

The action that I have announced tonight puts the leaders of North Vietnam on notice that we will be patient in working for peace, we will be conciliatory at the conference table, but we will not be humiliated. We will not be defeated. We will not allow American men by the thousands to be killed by an enemy from privileged sanctuaries.

# UNITED STATES NOTIFICATION TO THE UNITED NATIONS SECURITY COUNCIL OF SELF-DEFENSE MEASURES TAKEN BY THE UNITED STATES AND REPUBLIC OF VIET-NAM ARMED FORCES[1]

May 5, 1970

Dear Mr. President:

I have the honor to refer to the letters of February 7 and 27, 1965, from the Permanent Representative of the United States of America to the President of the Security Council concerning the aggression against the Republic of Viet-Nam and to inform you of the following acts of armed aggression by forces of North Viet-Nam based in Cambodia which have required appropriate measures of collective self-defense by the armed forces of the Republic of Viet-Nam and the United States of America.

For five years North Viet-Nam has maintained base areas in Cambodia against the expressed wishes of the Cambodian Government. These bases have been used in violation of Cambodian neutrality as supply points and base areas for military operations against the Republic of Viet-Nam. In recent weeks North Vietnamese forces have rapidly expanded the perimeters of these base areas and expelled the remaining Cambodian Government presence from the areas. The North Vietnamese forces have moved quickly to link the bases along the border with South Viet-Nam into one continuous chain as well as to push the bases deeper into Cambodia. Concurrently, North Viet-Nam has stepped up guerrilla actions into South Viet-Nam and concentrating its main forces in these base areas in preparation for further massive attacks into South Viet-Nam. These military actions against the Republic of Viet-Nam and its armed forces and the armed forces of the United States require appropriate defensive measures. In his address to the American people on April 30, President Nixon stated:

". . . If this enemy effort succeeds, Cambodia would become a vast enemy staging area and a springboard for attacks on South Viet-Nam along 600 miles of frontier: a refuge where enemy troops could return from combat without fear of retaliation.

"North Vietnamese men and supplies could then be poured into that country, jeopardizing not only the lives of our men but the people of South Viet-Nam as well."

---

[1] U.N. Doc. S/9781 (1970).

76

The measures of collective self-defense being taken by U.S. and South Vietnamese forces are restricted in extent, purpose and time. They are confined to the border areas over which the Cambodian Government has ceased to exercise any effective control and which has been completely occupied by North Vietnamese and Viet Cong forces. Their purpose is to destroy the stocks and communications equipment that are being used in aggression against the Republic of Viet-Nam. When that purpose is accomplished, our forces and those of the Republic of Viet-Nam will promptly withdraw. These measures are limited and proportionate to the aggressive military operations of the North Vietnamese forces and the threat they pose.

The United States wishes to reiterate its continued respect for the sovereignty, independence, neutrality, and territorial integrity of Cambodia. Our purpose in taking these defensive measures was stated by President Nixon, in his address of April 30, as follows:

"We take this action not for the purpose of expanding the war into Cambodia but for the purpose of ending the war in Viet-Nam, and winning the just peace we all desire.

"We have made and will continue to make every possible effort to end this war through negotiation at the conference table rather than through more fighting in the battlefield."

I would request that my letter be circulated to the Members of the Security Council.

Accept, Excellency, the assurances of my highest consideration.

CHARLES W. YOST
Permanent United States
Representative to the
United Nations.

His Excellency
    Jacques Kosciusko-Morizet,
        President of the Security Council.

# HATFIELD–McGOVERN:

## Amendment to the Military Procurement Bill, H.R. 17123

At an appropriate point in the bill insert the following:

"1. In accordance with public statements of policy by the President, no funds authorized by this or any other act may be obligated or expended to maintain a troop-level of more than 280,000 armed forces of the United States in Vietnam after April 30, 1971.

"2. After April 30, 1971, funds herein authorized or hereafter appropriated may be expended in connection with activities of American armed forces in and over Indochina only to accomplish the following objectives:

"(a) the orderly termination of military operations there and the safe and systematic withdrawal of remaining armed forces by December 31, 1971;

"(b) to secure the release of prisoners of war;

"(c) the provision of asylum for Vietnamese who might be physically endangered by withdrawal of American forces; and

"(d) to provide assistance to the Republic of Vietnam consistent with the foregoing objectives.

*"Provided, however,* That if the President while giving effect to the foregoing paragraphs of this section, finds in meeting the termination date that members of the American armed forces are exposed to unanticipated clear and present danger, he may suspend the application of paragraph 2(a) for a period of not to exceed 60 days and shall inform the Congress forthwith of his findings; and within 10 days following application of the suspension the President may submit recommendations, including (if necessary) a new date applicable to section 2(a) for Congressional approval."

# Bibliography

# Expansion of the Viet Nam War into Cambodia

## Selected Bibliography*

### Prepared by ANTHONY P. GRECH

*Librarian, The Association of the Bar
of the City of New York*

### GENERAL

Allison, Graham; May, Ernest and Yarmolinsky, Adam. Limits to intervention. 1970. 48 For. Aff. 245-61.

America's leading Asia scholars urge an end to the war. 116 Cong. Rec. S10382-S10386 (daily ed. June 30, 1970).

Bloomfield, L. P. International military forces; the question of peace-keeping in an armed and disarming world. Boston, Little, Brown. 1964. 296p.

Bromley, Dorothy. Washington and Vietnam; an examination of the moral and political issues. Dobbs Ferry, N.Y., Oceana. 1966. 120p.

Buchanan, Keith. Cambodia between Peking and Paris. 1964. 16 Monthly Rev. 480-92.

Cambodge. Gouvernement Royal. Livre jaune sur les revendications de l'indépendance du Cambodge. Vol. 1, Paris, Impr. Centrale Commerciale. 1953; Vol. 2, Phnom Penh, Impr. de Palais Royal. 1954.

Cambodia (bibliography). 25 J. Asian Studies 168-70 (Sept. 1966); 26:213-16 (Sept. 1967); 27:227-30 (Sept. 1968).

Canchy, de. Le Cambodge et la neutralité au sud-est asiatique. Oct. 1964. Rev. Militaire d' Information 62-69.

Chandler, David. Cambodia's strategy of survival. Dec. 1969. 57 Current Hist. 344.

Clifford, Clark M. A Viet Nam reappraisal. 1969. 47 For. Aff. 601-22.

Concern over Cambodian incursion. 116 Cong. Rec. S11710-S11713 (daily ed. July 20, 1970).

Couret, Bernard. Le Cambodge, prochaine victime de la guerre? July 23, 1966. Le Monde.

Deshpande, G. P. Cambodia and China — Cambodia's foreign policy is a product of history. Oct/Nov. 1966. 2 China Rep. (New Delhi) 16-20.

Doležal, Ivan. The policy of neutrality and the international position of Cambodia. 1969. Asian & African Studies 57-79.

Eckstein, Harry, ed. Internal war: problems and approaches. New York, Free Press. 1964. 339p.

*For materials prior to 1966 see bibliography in Tondel, Lyman M., ed.
The Southeast Asia Crisis . . . 8th Hammarskjöld Forum, Dobbs Ferry, Oceana, 1966, pp. 199-226.

Fresh danger in Cambodia. 116 Cong. Rec. S13115-S13118 (daily ed. August 11, 1970).

Gordon, B. K. Cambodia — shadow over Angkor. 1969. 9 Asian Survey 58-68.

Graber, D. A. Crisis diplomacy; a history of U.S. intervention policies and practices. Washington, Public Affairs Press. 1959. 402p.

Herz, Martin. A short history of Cambodia from the days of Angkor to the present. New York, Praeger. 1958. 141p.

Hoopes, Townsend. Legacy of the cold war in Indochina. 1970. 48 For. Aff. 601-66.

Hull, Roger H. The Paris accords. 1970. 56 A.B.A.J. 34-36.

Indochina. 116 Cong. Rec. S9198-S9202 (daily ed. June 17, 1970).

Les institutions du Cambodge. 1 Juillet 1969. Notes & Etudes Documentaires 1-40, no. 3605.

Johnson, Robert H. Vietnamization: can it work? 1970. 48 For. Aff. 629-47.

Kaplan, M. A. United States foreign policy in a revolutionary age. Princeton, Princeton Univ. Center of International Studies. 1961. 47p.

Lacouture, Jean. From the Vietnam war to an Indochina war. 1970. 48 For. Aff. 617-28.

Legal memorandum on the amendment to end the war. 116 Cong. Rec. S7477 (daily ed. May 19, 1970).

Leifer, Michael.
Cambodia; the search for security. New York, Praeger. 1967. 200p.
Cambodia and her neighbors. 1961/62. 34 Pac. Aff. 361-74.
Cambodia and SEATO. 1962. 17 Int'l J. 122-32.
Cambodia — in search of neutrality. Jan. 1963. 3 Asian Survey 55-60.
Cambodia looks to China. Jan. 1964. 20 World Today 26-31.
Cambodia — the politics of accommodation. 1964. 4 Asian Survey 674-79.
Cambodia — the limits of diplomacy. Jan. 1967. 7 Asian Survey 69-73.
The failure of political institutions in Cambodia. April 1968. 2 Mod. Asian Studies 131.
Rebellion or subversion in Cambodia? Feb. 1969. 56 Current Hist. 88-93.

Levi, Werner. Challenge of world politics in south and southeast Asia. Englewood Cliffs, N.J. 1968. 184p.

Liska, George. War and order: reflections on Vietnam and history. Baltimore, Johns Hopkins Press. 1968. 115p.

Marnas, L. Camboya — la raices y razones de una neutralidad. Marzo-Abril 1969. Revista de Politica Internacional 171-203.

Marsot, A. G. China's aid to Cambodia. 1969. 42 Pac. Aff. 189-98.

Murphy, Cornelius F., jr. Vietnam: a study of law and politics. 1968. 36 Fordham L. Rev. 453-60.

Osborne, M. E. Beyond charisma — princely politics and the problem of political succession in Cambodia. Winter 1968/69. 24 Int'l J. 109-21.

Osborne, Milton. Regional disunity in Cambodia. Dec. 1968. 22 Austl. Outlook 317-33.

Poole, Peter A. The Vietnamese in Thailand. Ithaca, Cornell Univ. Press. 1970. 180p.

President Nixon's report on Cambodia. 116 Cong. Rec. H6289-H6293 (daily ed. June 30, 1970); 116 Cong. Rec. S10533-S10537 (daily ed. July 1, 1970).

Recent developments in Cambodia. 116 Cong. Rec. S14689-S14691 (daily ed. Aug. 31, 1970).

Recent moves in Cambodian foreign policy: freewill or determinism? April 1966. 16 External Affairs Rev. (N.Z.) 3-13.

Sarkisyank, M. Die neutralität Kambodschas — ihre geschichte und ihr wesen. 1 Quartal 1969. 2 Verfassung und Recht in Ubersee 1-10.

Sihanouk, Norodom. Cambodia neutral: the dictate of necessity. 1958. 36 For. Aff. 582-86.

La monarchie cambodgienne et la croisade royale pour l' indépendance. Phnom Penh, Imprimerie Rasmey. 1961. 104p.

Smith, Roger M.

Cambodia — between Scylla and Charybdis. Jan. 1968. 8 Asian Survey 72-79.

Cambodia's foreign policy. Ithaca, Cornell Univ. Press. 1965. 273p.

Prince Norodom Sihanouk of Cambodia. June 1967. 7 Asian Survey 353-62.

Steinberg, David J. Cambodia, its people, its society, its culture. New Haven, HRAF Press. 1959. 351p.

Szaz, Zolton M. Cambodia's foreign policy. 1955. 24 Far E. Survey 151-58.

Tondel, Lyman M., ed. The Southeast Asia crisis. Background papers and proceedings of the eighth Hammarskjöld forum. Published for the Association of the Bar of the City of New York by Oceana Pub. 1966. 226p. (bibliography pp. 199-226).

U.S. Congress. Senate. Comm. on Foreign Relations.

(90.1) Background information to southeast Asia and Vietnam. 3d rev. ed. Washington, Gov't Print. Off. 1967. 308p.

(91.1) Briefing on Vietnam. Hearings . . . Nov. 18 & 19, 1969. Washington, Gov't Print. Off. 1969. 167p.

U.S. Dep't of the Army. Area handbook for Cambodia. Frederick P. Munsen and others. Washington, Gov't Print. Off. 1968. 364p. (DA PAM 550-50)

United States foreign policy for the 1970's (a report by President Nixon). H. doc. no. 258, 91st Cong., 2d sess (1970).

Williams, Maslyn. The land in between: the Cambodian dilemma. New York, Morrow. 1970. 241p.

Willmott, W. E. Cambodian neutrality. Jan. 1967. 52 Current Hist. 36-40, 52-53.

Young C. Le Cambodge sur la corde raide. 16-31 Juillet 1969. 21 Est et Ouest 20-24.

# CONSTITUTIONAL ASPECTS

Atkinson, J. D. Can the president send troops abroad: a review of the past and some calm advice on the crucial issue of presidential power. 1951. 26 Thought 117-27.

Bancroft, George. History of the formation of the constitution of the United States of America. 6th ed. New York, D. Appleton & Co. 1893. 2v.

Bassiouni, M. Cherif. The war power and the law of war: theory and realism. 1968. 18 De Paul L. Rev. 188-201.

Berdahl, Clarence A. War powers of the executive in the United States. Urbana, Ill., The Author. 1921. 296p.

Brinkley, Wilfred E.

The man in the white house: his powers and duties. Rev. ed. New York, Harper & Row. 1964. 274p.

The powers of the president; problems of American democracy. New York, Doubleday. 1937. 332p.

President and congress. 3d rev. ed. New York, Vintage Books. 1962. 403p.

Boutwell, George S. The constitution of the United States at the end of the first century. Boston, D. C. Heath. 1896. 412p.

Bradshaw, Mary E. Congress and foreign policy since 1900. 1953. 289 Annals 40-48.

Brown, Ben H., Jr. Congress and the department of state. 1953. 289 Annals 100-07.

The Cambodian invasion (University of Kansas law school). 116 Cong. Rec. S8305 (daily ed. June 13, 1970).

Carras, William G. The analysis and interpretation of the use of presidential authority to order United States armed forces into military action in foreign territories without a formal declaration of war. Ann Arbor, University Microfilms. (Microfilm AC-1, no. 60-1084).

Carroll, Holbert N. The house of representatives and foreign affairs. Pittsburgh, Univ. of Pittsburgh Press. 1958. 365p.

Cheever, Daniel S. and Haviland, H. Field. American foreign policy and the separation of powers. Cambridge, Harvard Univ. Press. 1952. 244p.

Chiperfield, Robert B. The committee on foreign affairs. 1953. 289 Annals 73-83.

Cohen, Benjamin V. The evolving role of congress in foreign affairs. 1948. 92 Proc. Am. Phil. Soc'y 211-16.

Congress, the president, and the power to commit forces to combat. 1968. 81 Harv. L. Rev. 1771-1805.

Constitutional symposium on Indochina war. 116 Cong. Rec. S7966 (daily ed. May 28, 1970).

Corwin, Edward S.

The constitution and what it means today. Princeton, Princeton Univ. Press. 1958. 344p.

The president, office and powers, 1787-1957; history and analysis of practice and opinion. 4th rev. ed. New York, New York Univ. Press. 1957. 519p.

The president's control of foreign relations. Princeton, Princeton Univ. Press. 1917.

Who has the power to make war? N.Y. Times Mag., July 31, 1949, pp. 11, 14, 15.

Corwin, Edward S. and Peltason, J. W. Understanding the constitution. 4th ed. New York, Holt, Rinehart & Winston. 1967. 200p.

Crosskey, William W. Politics and the constitution in the history of the United States. Chicago, Univ. of Chicago Press. 1953. (Vol. 1, pp. 416-17, 422, 28, 510-11)

Curtis, George Tichnor.
  Constitutional history of the United States. New York, Harper & Bros.
    1889. (Vol. 1, pp. 463, 527, 552, 576-79)
  History of the origin, formation and adoption of the constitution of the
    United States. New York, Harper & Bros. 1863. (Vol. 2, pp. 231, 332,
    413)
Dahl, Robert A. Congress and foreign policy. New York, Harcourt, Brace.
  1950. 305p.
Dennison, Eleanor E. The senate foreign relations committee. Stanford, Stan-
  ford Univ. Press. 1942.
Dumbauld, Edward. The constitution of the United States. Norman, Univ. of
  Oklahoma Press. 1964. (pp. 163-70, 279-82)
Editorial support for the amendment to end the war. 116 Cong. Rec.
  S9190-9192 (daily ed. June 17, 1970)
Egger, Rowland A. and Harris, Joseph P. The president and congress. New
  York, McGraw-Hill. 1963. 128p.
Faulkner, Stanley. The war in Vietnam: is it constitutional? 1968. 56 Geo. L.
  J. 1132-43.
Foley, Edward H., jr. Some aspects of the constitutional powers of the presi-
  dent. 1941. 27 A.B.A.J. 485-90.
Franklin, Mitchell. War power of the president. 1942. 17 Tul. L. Rev. 217-55.
Fulbright, J. William. American foreign policy in the 20th century under an
  18th century constitution. 1961. 47 Cornell L.Q. 1-13.
Gillette, Guy M. The senate in foreign relations. 1953. 289 Annals 49-57.
Goebel, Dorothy B. Congress and foreign relations before 1900. 1953. 289
  Annals 22-39.
Griffith, Ernest S.
  Congress; its contemporary role. 3d ed. New York, New York Univ. Press.
    1961. 243p.
  The place of congress in foreign relations. 1953. 289 Annals 11-21.
Haight, David E. and Johnston, Larry D., eds. The president, roles and
  powers. Chicago, Rand McNally. 1965. 400p.
Haviland, Henry F. The formulation and administration of United States
  foreign policy. Washington, Brookings Institution. 1960. 191p.
Henkin, Louis.
  Constitutional issues in foreign policy. 1969. 23 J. Int'l Aff. 210-24.
  Viet-Nam in the courts of the United States — "political questions." 1969.
    63 Am. J. Int'l L. 284-89.
Hilsman, Roger. Congressional-executive relations and the foreign policy con-
  sensus. 1958. 52 Am. Pol. Sci. Rev. 725-44.
Hirschfield, Robert S. The power of the presidency. New York, Atherton
  Press. 1968. 328p.
Hockett, Homer C. The constitutional history of the United States,
  1776-1876. New York, Macmillan. 1939. 2v.
Holcombe, Arthur N. Our more perfect union; from eighteenth-century prin-
  ciples to twentieth-century practice. Canbridge, Harvard Univ. Press. 1950.
  460p.
Holst, Hermann Eduard, von. The constitutional and political history of the
  United States. Chicago, Callaghan. 1881/1882. 8v.

83

Houghton, Neal D. War-making and the constitution: expansion of presidential and Pentagonal war-making proclivities in recent decades. April 1964. 39 Soc. Sci. 67-78.

Huzar, Elias. The purse and the sword: control of the army by congress through military appropriations 1933-1950. Ithaca, Cornell Univ. Press. 1950. 417p.

Hyman, Sidney. The American president. New York, Harper. 1954. 342p.

Indochina: the constitutional crisis. 116 Cong. Rev. S7117 (daily ed. May 13, 1970); 116 Cong. Rec. S7591 (daily ed. May 21, 1970).

Javits, Jacob K. The congressional presence in foreign relations. 1970. 48 For. Aff. 221-34.

Jones, Harry W. The president, congress and foreign relations. 1941. 29 Calif. L. Rev. 565-85.

Koening, Louis W.
The chief executive. New York, Harcourt, Brace and World. 1964. 435p.
The presidency and the crisis. Powers of the office from the invasion of Poland to Pearl Harbor. New York, Kings Crown Press. 1944. 166p.

McConnell, Grant. The modern presidency. New York, St. Martin's Press. 1967. 114p.

McLaughlin, Andrew Cunningham. A constitutional history of the United States. New York, London, D. Appleton-Century. 1936. 843p.

Malawer, Stuart S. The Vietnam war under the constitution: legal issues involved in the United States military involvement in Vietnam. 1969. 31 U. Pitt. L. Rev. 205-41.

May, Ernest R. The ultimate decision: the president as commander in chief. New York, George Braziller. 1960. 200p.

Meeker, Leonard C. The legality of United States participation in the defense of Viet-Nam. 1966. 54 Dep't State Bull. 474-89.

Milton, George F. The use of presidential power 1780-1943. Boston, Little, Brown. 1944. (Chap. 6, Commander in chief, pp. 107-22)

*Mora v. McNamara,* 389 U.S. 934 (1967), United States supreme court order denying review as to legality of United States military actions in Viet-Nam; relation of the courts to the executive branch. 1968. 7 Int'l Leg. Materials 18-21.
*also* Petition for writ of certiorari to the United States court of appeals for the District of Columbia circuit. 35p. (Oct. term 1967 no. 401) and Memorandum for the respondents in opposition. (Oct. term 1967 no. 401) 5p.

Morgan, Donald Grant. Congress and the constitution; a study of responsibility. Cambridge, Belknap Press of Harvard Univ. Press. 1966. pp. 183, 204-17.

Morison, Samuel E. and Commager, Henry Steele. The growth of the American republic. 4th ed. rev. & enl. New York, Oxford Univ. Press. 1950. 2v.

Morris, Richard B. Great presidential decisions; state papers that changed the course of history. Greenwich, Conn., Fawcett Pub. 1966. 469p.

Nanes, Allan S. Congress and military commitments: an overview. 1969. 57 Current Hist. 105.

Ogul, Morris S. Reforming executive-legislative relations in the conduct of American foreign policy: the executive-legislative council as a proposed solution. Ann Arbor, University Microlfilms. 1958. (Microfilm AC-1, no. 58-3717)

Poole, De Witt C. The conduct of foreign relations under modern democratic conditions. New Haven, Published for the Institute of Politics by Yale Univ. Press. 1924. 208p.

Potter, Pitman B. The power of the president of the United States to utilize its armed forces abroad. 1954. 48 Am J. Int'l L. 458-59.

Prescott, Arthur T. Drafting the federal constitution. University, Louisiana State Univ. Press. 1941. (pp. 513-17)

Pritchett, Charles H. The American constitution. New York, McGraw-Hill. 1959. (pp. 344-63)

Pusey, Merlo J.
   Law of the land and the war power. 116 Cong. Rec. S8751 (daily ed. June 10, 1970).
   The way we go to war. Boston, Houghton, Mifflin. 1969. 202p.

Reveley, W. Taylor, III. Presidential war-making: constitutional prerogative or usurpation? 1969. 55 Va. L. Rev. 1243-1305.

Richards, James P. The house of representatives in foreign affairs. 1953. 289 Annals 66-72.

Robinson, Edgar E. Powers of the president in foreign affairs 1945-1965. San Francisco, Commonwealth Club of California. 1966. 279p.

Rogers, James G. World policing and the constitution; an inquiry into the powers of the president and congress, nine wars and a hundred military operations, 1789-1945. Boston, World Peace Foundation. 1945. 123p. (America looks ahead series, no. 11)

Rossiter, Clinton L. The American presidency. 2d ed. New York, Harcourt, Brace. 1960. 281p.

Rostow, Eugene V. et al. Letter on constitutional authority of president in using American troops. 116 Cong. Rec. S8404 (daily ed. June 4, 1970).

Schwartz, Bernard. A commentary on the constitution of the United States, Pt. I, The powers of government. New York, Macmillan. 1963. (Vol. 2, War power, pp. 170-305)

Schwartz, Warren F. and McCormack, Wayne. The justiciability of legal objections to the American military effort in Vietnam. 1968. 46 Texas L. Rev. 1033-53.

Schwarzer, William W. and Wood, Robert R. Presidential power and aggression abroad. 1954. 40 A.B.A.J. 394-97.

Smith, Louis. American democracy and military power. A study of civil control of military power in the United States. Chicago, Univ. of Chicago Press. 1951. 370p.

Sparkman, John. Changing concepts of control of the armed forces. 1957. 61 Dick. L. Rev. 335-44.

Standard, William L. United States intervention is not legal. 1966. 52 A.B.A.J. 627-34.

Story, Joseph. Commentaries on the constitution of the United States. 5th ed. Boston, Little, Brown. 1905, 1891. 2v.

Sutherland, George. Constitutional power and world affairs. New York, Columbia Univ. Press. 1919. 202p.

Swisher, Carl B. American constitutional development. 2d ed. Boston, Houghton, Mifflin. 1954. 1145p.

U.S. Cong. House. Comm. on Foreign Affairs. (82.1) Back-ground information on the use of United States forces in foreign countries. Report prepared by George Lee Millikan and Sheldon Z. Kaplan . . . pursuant to H. Res. 28, a resolution authorizing the Committee on foreign affairs to conduct thorough studies and investigations of all matters coming within the jurisdiction of such committee. Washington, Gov't Print. Off. 1951. 77p.

U. S. Cong. House. Comm. on Foreign Affairs. Subcom. on National Security Policy and Scientific Developments. (91.2) Congress, the president and the war powers. Hearings . . . June 18, 23, 24, 25, 30, July 1, 9, 23, 28, 30 and Aug. 5, 1970. Washington, Gov't Print. Off. 1970.

U.S. Congress. Senate. Comm. on Foreign Relations. Powers of the president to send the armed forces outside the United States, prepared for the use of the joint committee made up of the Committee on foreign relations and Committee on armed services of the senate. Washington, Gov't Print. Off. 1951. 27p.

U.S. Constitutional Convention, 1787. The records of the federal convention of 1787; edited by Max Farrand. Rev. ed. New Haven, Yale Univ. Press. 1937. 4v.

U.S. Library of Congress. Legislative Reference Service. The powers of the president as commander in chief of the army and navy of the United States. Prepared at the request of John W. McCormack . . . by Dorothy Schaffer . . . and Dorothy M. Mathews. Washington, Gov't Print. Off. 1956. 145p.

U.S. Library of Congress. Legislative Reference Service. Foreign Affairs Div. Background information on the use of United States armed forces in foreign countries. 1970 rev. Washington, Gov't Print. Off. 1970. 62p.

Velvel, Lawrence R. The war in Viet Nam: unconstitutional, justiciable and jurisdictionally attackable. 1968. 16 Kan. L. Rev. 449-503(e).

Warren, Charles. The making of the constitution. Boston, Little, Brown. 1928. 832p.

Watkins, A.V. War by executive order. 1951. 4 W. Pol. Q. 539-49.

Westphal, Albert C. F. The house committee on foreign affairs. New York, Columbia Univ. Press. 1942. 263p.

White Malcolm K. The war powers of the president. 1943. Wis. L. Rev. 205-28.

Wiley, Alexander. The committee on foreign relations. 1953. 289 Annals 58-65.

Wise, Sidney and Schier, Richard F., eds. The presidential office. New York, Crowell. 1968. 248p.

Wormuth, F. The Vietnam war: the president versus the constitution (Occasional paper: Center for the Study of Democratic Institutions). April 1968.

Worsnop, Richard L.
Presidential power. Oct. 2, 1968. Editorial Res. Rep. 723-40.
War powers of the president. March 14, 1966. Editorial Res. Rep. 183-200.

Wright, Quincy. The control of American foreign relations. New York, Macmillan. 1922. 412p.

Alford, Neil H., jr. The legality of American military involvement in Viet Nam: a broader perspective. 1966. 75 Yale L.J. 1109-21.

Barnet, Richard J. Patterns of intervention (In Falk, R.A., ed. The Vietnam war and international law, v.2, pp. 1162-75, Princeton, 1969)

Bender, John C. Self-defense and Cambodia: a critical appraisal. Oct. 19, 1970. 164 N.Y.L.J. 1,4; Oct. 20, 1970. 164 N.Y.L.J. 1,4.

Bowett, D. W. Self-defense in international law. New York, Praeger. 1958. 294p.

Brownlie, Ian. International law and the use of force by states. Oxford, Clarendon Press. 1963. 532p.

Cambodian invasion and international law (Columbia law school). 116 Cong. Rec. E4571 (daily ed. May 21, 1970); 116 Cong. Rec. E5228 (daily ed. June 4, 1970).

Castrén, Erik Johannes Sukari. The present law of war and neutrality. Helsinki. 1954. 630p.

Curtis, Roy Emerson. The law of hostile military expeditions as applied by the United States. 1914. 8 Am. J. Int'l L. 1-37.

Deutsch, Eberhard P.
Legality of the war in Vietnam. 1968. 7 Washburn L. J. 153-86.
The legality of the United States position in Vietnam. 1966. 52 A.B.A.J. 436-42.

Falk, Richard A.
International law and the United States role in the Viet Nam war. 1966. 75 Yale L. J. 1123-60.
International law and the United States role in Viet Nam: a response to Professor Moore. 1967. 76 Yale L. J. 1095-1158.
Legal order in a violent world. Princeton, Princeton Univ. Press. 1968. 610p.
United States foreign policy and the Vietnam war: a second American dilemma. 1968. 3 Stanford J. Int'l Studies 78-98.

Falk, Richard A., ed. The Vietnam war and international law. Princeton, Princeton Univ. Press. 1968. (sponsored by American society of international law) 633p.

Farer, Tom J.
Intervention in civil wars: a modest proposal. 1967. 67 Colum. L. Rev. 266-79.
Problems of an international law of intervention. 1968. 3 Stanford J. Int'l Studies 20-26.

Fenwick, Charles G. Intervention: individual and collective. 1945. 39 Am. J. Int'l L. 645-63.

Firmage, Edwin B. International law and the response of the United States to "internal war." 1967. Utah L. Rev. 517-46.

Friedmann, Wolfgang G.
Commentary on "United States intervention: doctrine and practice." 1968. 3 Stanford J. Int'l Studies 107-13.
Law and politics in the Vietnamese war; a comment. 1967. 61 Am. J. Int'l L. 776-85.

Greenspan, Morris. The modern law of land warfare. Berkeley, Univ. of California Press. 1959. 724p.

Guggenheim, Paul. Traité de droit international public. Genève, Georg.

Halpern, Manfred. The morality and politics of intervention. New York, Council on Religion and International Affairs. 1963. 36p.

Henkin, Louis. Force, intervention and neutrality in contemporary (In Falk, Richard A. & Mendlovitz, Saul H., eds. International law. N.Y., World Law Fund, pp. 335-52)

Hershey, Amos S. Incursions into Mexico and the doctrine of hot pursuit. 1919. 13 Am. J. Int'l L. 557-69.

Hull, Roger H. and Novogrod, John C. Law and Vietnam. Foreword by Myres S. McDougal. Dobbs Ferry, N.Y., Oceana. 1968. 211p.

International Commission for Supervision and Control in Cambodia. 1st progress report, Jan. 1, 1955. London, H.M. Stat. Off. 1955-.

International law and military operations against insurgents in neutral territory. 1968. 68 colum. L. Rev. 1127-48.

Invasion of Cambodia violates international law: N.Y.U. law students brief, 116 Cong. Rec. E4443 (daily ed. May 19, 1970); 116 Cong. Rec. S7823 (daily ed. May 26, 1970).

Joint communique (Cambodia & U.S.), Jan. 12, 1968. 1968. 58 Dep't State Bull. 133-34.

Kaplan, Morton A. and Katzenbach, Nicholas deB. Resort to force: war and neutrality (In Falk, Richard A. & Mendlovitz, Saul H., eds. International law. N.Y., World Law Fund, pp. 276-306)

Komarnicki, Titus. The place of neutrality in the modern system of international law (In Hague. Academie de droit international. Recueil des cours 1952, I, vol. 80, pp. 397-510)

Lacouture, Jean. From the Vietnam war to an Indochina war. 1970. 48 For. Aff. 617-28.

Legality of the United States involvement in Vietnam — a pragmatic approach. 1969. 23 U. Miami L. Rev. 792.

The legality of United States participation in the defense of Viet-Nam. 1966. 60 Am. J. Int'l L. 565-85.

Manning, Bayless. Foreign intervention in civil strife: from diplomacy to politics. 1968. 3 Stanford J. Int'l Studies 1-4.

Margolis, Emanuel. Escalating the Viet Nam debate — a reply to professor Moore. 1968. 42 Conn. B.J. 23-54.

Meeker, Leonard C.
  Law and policy in Viet Nam. 1966. 38 Pa. B.A.Q. 21-26.
  The legality of United States participation in the defense of Viet-Nam. 1966. 54 Dep't State Bull. 474-89.

Messing, John H. American actions in Vietnam: justifiable in international law? 1967. 19 Stanford L. Rev. 1307-36.

Modelski, George. The international relations of internal war. Princeton, Center for International Studies. 1961. 24p.

Moore, John Norton.
  International law and the United States role in Viet Nam: a reply. 1967. 76 Yale L.J. 1051-94.
  The role of law in the Viet Nam debate. 1967. 41 Conn. B.J. 389-401.

Moore, John Norton and Underwood, James L. The lawfulness of United States assistance to the Republic of Viet Nam. 1966/67. 5 Duquesne U. L. Rev. 235.

Morris, David J. Commentary on "United States intervention: doctrine and practice." 1968. 3 Stanford J. Int'l Studies 114-21.

Oppenheim, L. International law. 7th ed. by Hersh Lauterpacht. London, Longmans, Green. 1952. (Vol. 2, Disputes, war and neutrality)

Partan, Daniel G. Legal aspects of the Vietnam conflict. 1966. 46 B.U.L. Rev. 281-316.

Poulantzas, Nicholas M. The right of hot pursuit in international law. Leyden, Sijthoff. 1969. 451p.

Robertson, David W. The debate among American international lawyers about the Vietnam war. 1968. 46 Texas L. Rev. 898-913.

Rogers, William D. United States intervention: doctrine and practice. 1968. 3 Stanford J. Int'l Studies 99-106.

Schick, F. B. Some reflections on the legal controversies concerning America's involvement in Vietnam. 1968. 17 Int'l & Comp. L.Q. 953-95.

Schwartz, Warren F. and McCormack, Wayne. The justiciability of legal objections to the American military effort in Vietnam. 1968. 46 Texas Rev. 1033-53.

Stone, Julius. Legal controls of international conflict; a treatise on the dynamics of disputes and war-law. 2d impression rev. with supplement, 1953-1958. New York, Rinehart. 1959. 903p.

Stowell, Ellery C. Intervention in international law. Washington, John Byrne Co. 1921. 558p.

United Nations. Security Council. Resolution on Cambodian-Vietnamese frontier. 1964. 3 Int'l Leg. Materials 792.

United States: the Cambodian incursion. Letter to U.N. security council informing of action . . . Statement on issues of international law involved in U.S. military actions . . . Staff report of senate foreign relations committee concerning events before and after incursion. 1970. 9 Int'l Leg. Materials 838-71.

U.S. Dep't of State, Office of the Legal Adviser. The legality of United States participation in the defense of Viet Nam. 1966. 75 Yale L.J. 1085-1108.

U.S. releases note to Cambodia on violations of its territory. Jan. 22, 1968. 58 Dep't State Bull. 124.

Whiteman, Marjorie M. Digest of international law. Washington, Gov't Print. Off. 1968. (Vols. 10 & 11)

Williams, Glanville L. The judicial basis of hot pursuit. 1939. 20 Brit. Yb. Int'l L. 83-97.

Winfield, P. H. The history of intervention in international law. 1922/23. 3 Brit. Yb. Int'l L. 130-49.

Wright, Quincy. Legal aspects of the Viet-Nam situation. 1966. 60 Am. J. Int'l L. 750-69.

89

## DATE DUE

| MAR 6 '80 | MAR 6 '80 | | |
|-----------|-----------|--|--|
|           |           |  |  |
|           |           |  |  |
|           |           |  |  |
|           |           |  |  |
|           |           |  |  |
|           |           |  |  |
|           |           |  |  |
|           |           |  |  |
|           |           |  |  |
|           |           |  |  |
|           |           |  |  |
|           |           |  |  |
| GAYLORD   |           |  | PRINTED IN U.S.A. |